Copyright © 2024 by Louna Stone
Book cover design by Louna Stone and Mixo
Prosthetic engravement design

All characters, establishm
publication, other than clearly
fictitious and any resemblanc
dead, is purely coincidental.

All rights reserved.
No part of this publication may be reproduced or distributed in any form without prior written permission from the author, with the exception of non-commercial uses permitted by copyright law. No part of this book may be reproduced or transmitted by any means, except as permitted by UK copyright law or the author.
Quotes, images and information may be used for book reviews and social media posts.
For licensing requests, please contact the author at LounaStoneAuthor@hotmail.com.

Please note that this book is written under poetic license and therefore facts and the storyline may not be factually correct. They are written for entertainment purposes only.

www.LounaStone.com

Introduction and content trigger warnings

Dear reader, I hope you're having a lovely day. Thanks for picking up my book and joining me on this scary but exciting journey. I appreciate you very much.

Just a quick note that there are some topics in this book that may be **triggering**. The story includes sexual harassment, abuse, disability, mental illness and open sex scenes. Discretion is advised.

I have done research into the topics where I have little experience, so I hope I have done them justice and represented them the best way possible.

If any of the scenes make you feel uncomfortable or triggered, please put the book down and take care of yourself by speaking to someone about your struggles. You matter.

Playlist note:

Throughout the book there will be a different song for each chapter. The songs may or may not represent the storyline, but I chose them to help with the overall vibe of the chapters themselves to help some with their reading experience. I'm aware that this is not accessible to some, therefore the songs are not necessary to the enjoyment or experience of the book overall, just a little addition. You can search each song or head to the playlist on YouTube and Spotify called 'Love, in balance Playlist'. You can listen to these songs or read the lyrics before, whilst or after you read each chapter, or just anytime that works for you best. I love all of the songs so much. I hope you enjoy!

Love, In Balance

Five Mountains series
Book 1

Louna Stone

Louna Stone

To those who find that books bring them balance. This is for you.

Dear reader,

Thank you for picking up my book. This is the first edition. There is a new and improved edition on Amazon now!

Louna
x

Prologue

Lista
Playlist: *The Lakes* – Taylor Swift

I'm currently in the countryside with four of my closest friends, who all happen to be men.
And no, none of them are even close to being a love interest of mine. I love them, but my goodness do they get on my nerves at times.

With all being academics, we love taking time away and just resting our noggins.

Working in STEM can take its toll on you, so we all need to recharge our batteries and minds for when we return to the University and our everyday lives.

Reed was a fellow student like me, but he's just left and used his literature degree to open his own bookshop. Whilst Drew, Si and Pip are in various degrees of teaching. Drew is in computer engineering, Si in Chemistry, and Pip is the Design Technology buff.

And then there's me, a nerdy, petite girl in my second year of a PhD in engineering; focusing on biomechanical engineering, to be specific.

Love, In Balance

This weekend, despite the snow, I've hiked, taken insanely beautiful scenic walks and somehow managed the steep hills better than the guys, despite walking on my newly fitted transtibial prosthesis that I've been breaking in for just over a month.

I guess the workouts, vestibular exercises and physio have been paying off.

Plus I do have my trusty cane too, I suppose.

His name is Støtte. He's my first and only love up to this point. He's quite literally the balance in my life. If you tell me it's just a cane, I will disagree until the cows come home!

We rented out an Airbnb in The Lake District, and it's been the nicest way to spend the rest of the year.

I truly have had moments feeling like a Jane Austen Character whilst walking and taking in the scenic views; And have embodied Amanda Woods from The Holiday whilst being curled up in front of the fire with a book in the Airbnb. Both minus a gorgeous, charming gentlemen, however. Besides Støtte.

I mean, I suppose I'm lucky to have four charming gents here with me, but it's just not the same.

I need my Mr Darcy, ok!? I need the kind of romance where you have those *bend the knee* kisses. You know those cliché ones, where the kiss is so good that you bend one leg back and it looks cute AF. Yeah, that's what I'm after. Plus, the average folk takes the ability to bend their knees for granted; I had to re-learn how to do that after my amputation. Plus bending my knee for long periods can cause big issues for below the knee amputees so, I want at least one special moment.

This evening we're heading to a country pub that Reed picked.

He's the trips organiser and father figure of the group (despite being one of the youngest), so we heavily rely on him to be responsible for choosing good places to visit that have vegan options for little old me.

So far, so good.

He's even recommended a nice walking route for me to take solo today before we need to get ready to head to the pub.

So I fully intend on taking every opportunity to romanticise it and act like I'm an elegant lady from the 1800's with Elizabeth Bennet type attire.

I do not however own any form of such clothing, so I'll just imagine it, whilst wearing my very average leggings, thermal long-sleeved T-shirt, docs and the cosiest, warming cardigan.

I've even packed a cute little copy of Pride and Prejudice in my backpack for some cute countryside pictures and a little reading session. Providing I don't freeze my tits off.

What's the point in living if you can't romanticise the little things that life gives. Reading, sat underneath a beautiful tree in the countryside is the most perfect thing to do, and I intend to do it. And we're blessed with the snow too. It's the most beautiful place to see covered in a frosty, sparkling layer of white.

The guys are doing their own things today; Reed is enjoying reading, in between taking calls about his store, and Drew is playing video games with Pip and Si. Hence why I've decided to take this opportunity to welcome solitude and get some headspace before a busy evening.

The walk was divine, *thank you for asking*.

It well and truly refreshed me and gave me chance to get used to different surfaces on my leg. Win, win.

I'm feeling strong on it already. And braving the snow was a huge deal too. Go me!

Despite doing so well on my new prosthetic, my residual leg muscles get sore, especially after a walk in the snow, and so it's important to give my body time to rest. The last time I quite literally ran before I could walk; my prosthetist handed me my arse on a plate.

I'd only been trying out my first leg for a few months and pushed myself too far, resulting in taking ten steps back in my both my physical, mental and emotional recovery.

Trust me, I listened to him and actually learned that time. Since then, I've followed the guidance he's given to me like my life depended on it, because I've come to realise that in a way, it kind of does.

In order to soothe my muscles and let my leg rest, ready for the evening, I take my health teams advice and remove my gorgeous lower leg when I get home from walking.

She deserves rest too.

I use my crutches to get around. It took a long time to adapt to this new way of life for me, but as I got older I realised how capable we are of doing so; adapting during difficult times that we thought would be the end of us. It turns out, it was just the beginning. When I truly lost everything that mattered to me, I had no idea I could grow and find my purpose in life.

I took a super lovely shower when I settled back into the Airbnb from my walk and was able to take my time thanks to having an accessible ensuite all to myself. Otherwise the guys would be queuing up for their turn and shouting at me to hurry up. I'd end up with one armpit and one leg unshaved.

And if you think I'm joking, I'm not. They rushed me so much before, I got overwhelmed and ended up leaving the house half clean shaven and half like a baby yeti.

Yes, It's my own fault. I take ages showering.

But in my defence, I have long hair, balance issues, one full length leg to balance on in the slippery conditions, as opposed to the average two, and I enjoy the warm embrace of hot water on my skin, especially when it's freezing outside.

It's like a comforting cuddle, and a space just for me to feel at ease.

I get out of the shower with enough time to calmly get dressed, dry my hair and put some makeup on. I even light some scented candles and sip some mulled wine too.

Talk about living life. *This* girl is fucking content.

For our little outing this evening, I decided to go with some short black dungarees, tights (of course), a cosy black long sleeved top and a burgundy, soft, thick cardigan alongside my black boots.

I paired it with a chunky faux wool black scarf because oh my, it is soooo cold outside.

I've even blessed fellow humans by wearing a padded bra, but if I'm being honest, it's actually just so that my nips don't freeze.

Chapter 1

Lista

Playlist: *Is it New Years Yet* – Sabrina Carpenter

"I'm going to the bar" I say flatly to the table of pumped-up men I happen to be sitting with.

Well, I don't happen to be sat with them. They are my best friends, most of the time, so it was very much so a choice to be here, sharing a table. *I digress.*

Every once in a while, I need some breathing room, and since they forgot some of the drinks order, this is my cue for said breathing room.

It's New Year's Eve. I'm in the cosiest little country pub (Reed chose wisely), doing a special pub quiz, and couldn't be happier to be spending it this way. I know what you're thinking. *Boring.* But this is us. We are a group of academics. Need I say more?

We decided this year to hire an Airbnb in the countryside and spend the last days of December hiking, playing board games and doing an epic pub quiz, despite missing a few of the group members, therefore slightly less brain power.

Not for you? Fair enough.

We aren't the type for clubs or loud parties, where you can only rely on body language to be able to communicate. Plus trying to avoid having drink spilt on you by hammered partiers.

So here we are, in the lake district, in a small pub, celebrating with the locals.

It's nice being away from home.

There's something about being somewhere new that refreshes and rejuvenates my soul. Far away from the pressures of everyday life, with like-minded friends who deeply understand the need to escape. This is the perfect way to end the year and begin a new one.

I call to order my drink at the bar at the same time as a man further down does. We look at each other and laugh briefly before he signals for the bar tender to serve me first. *I didn't realise Gentlemen still existed. Or in fact, just kind people. Chivalry isn't in fact dead!*

After thanking him silently with a nod and smile, I order my drink and pay. He does so after me.

"It might take me a few minutes folks. I'm a little backed up with orders. Please bear with me" the middle-aged bar woman says.

"Please take your time. There's no rush" I reassure her.

I've realised during life that everyone is just trying to get by, so having patience and showing kindness is the least I can do to make someone's day that bit easier or brighter. *Unless they're being a shithead. Simple.*

The bar is swarming with cheerful older men and women talking loudly to one another and laughing.

It's overwhelming for my sensitive ears, but I can see how

joyful they are, and it helps me through it. Plus, I have my handy loop ear plugs in, so that makes things easier.

I think they're locals based on their accents, so I focus on the rhythm of their speech to help my mind concentrate on one thing instead of the cluster of noises and visual distractions.

You see, since the car accident during my childhood, I become easily overwhelmed and off balance due to my head injury. And my senses are... well, sensitive. If I get too overwhelmed or stressed, the vertigo is triggered, and when that happens, it's kind of game over for my productivity or fun. And let's face it. My quiz team need me. So prevention is vital for me.

I'm lost in thought, subconsciously eavesdropping on the local's chatter, when I get plucked out of my head and brought back to the real world.

"Sorry but have we met?", a deep male voice to my right says. I look up and see it's the man from down the bar, talking to me.

My heart begins racing. I've forgotten how to speak.

"Erm, I'm not sure".

It's not every day that a strikingly handsome man sparks up conversation with me, so I'm a little taken by surprise. But it hits me that upon closer inspection, I do feel like I've seen him before. Then again, it would be hard not to see him with his short black ruffled hair, dark eyes, and tall stature. His sharp jaw line, stubble and defined cheek bones make him impossibly handsome, but not too clean cut and model like. Still a hint of rugged, geekiness *(Is that a word? Yes. It is. I googled it)*

"Actually, I do feel like I've seen you somewhere. I'm not from around here though" I say, for some reason, disappointed.

"Oh, neither am I. I'm Just here for New Year's Eve with some mates" he says. His voice is smooth, deep and elegant. I'm intrigued. I'm also pleased to know he's *also* not local.
Maybe we *have* bumped into each other before.

"Ha snap!" I say as I point over to the group of hyped-up men, who appear to be very passionately discussing something I can't make out from here. I do love them.

Before either of us could say anything, my very considerate quiz team, which we collectively decided to call '*Five mountains*' (as always) demand me to return to the table. *Five mountains* is our friends group name. *Long* story. I came along post name discovery, so, not my doing.

"Lista! Come back over. The quiz is about to start back up". I signal to them that I'm still waiting for my drink, which brings a collective sigh to my entire table.
They take pub quizzes very seriously. Being academics takes its toll on us, I think. A loud voice comes through the speakers, and I jump a little.

"This next round is a little trickier folks so get your thinking caps on" the quiz master announces.

I get multiple sets of glares from the table of impatient men I call my friends. I mime that I'll be there as soon as possible, with a hint of aggression to my face and body language. *If you'd actually remembered my drink I wouldn't be up here now, would I?*

Love, In Balance

"Question one. Who was the first woman to earn a degree in MIT's electrical engineering department in 1918, who also invented the graphical calculator?".

Before I even have time to process what is happening, myself and the man I've had minimal conversation with both shout out the answer simultaneously "Edith Clarke".

"Correct".

Yeah, no shit. We both look at each other with raised eyebrows, until the next question comes along.

"Question two, what "D" word refers to the weight per unit volume of any given substance? Back to the futures film character George McFly tells Lorraine that she is his…". *Another easy one.*

"Density" We both shout out again.

Looks like I've met my match. And he is glorious.
He's either a fellow academic or likes Back to the future. Either way, he's making my insides twirl.

"Correct" is shouted out loudly and pulls me from my admiration of bar guy. My teammates look at me with equal disgust and appreciation as I give them no time to answer the questions themselves. I'm starting to think that bar guy and I should probably create our own little alliance. Great minds think alike.

"I'm actually going to give the lads a chance to answer this time. You know, help with their egos and all" I say to my new quiz companion.

He agrees.

"I'll try and hold back to see how both our teams get on without us then" he says, winking at me. Game on.

"Question four, is it true or false that Iron is attracted by magnets?"

This time, instead of calling out the answer, bar guy and I quietly whisper the answer.

"True"

Both correct again. Luckily my team called out the right answer too. Another point for us. Yes! (*A silent victory*). Oh shit, maybe I also take pub quizzes too seriously. Well in my defence, if they involve anything relating to science or engineering, that's when I'm as hooked as a child is to some bizarre trippy kids show on TV these days. To be honest, I wouldn't have minded losing to bar guy though. He seems nice.

Disappointingly, the flustered bar lady has now served our drinks, so my excuses to stay stood here with this like-minded stranger dwindle.

One more question and I'll retreat to my team.

"Question five, how many millilitres are there in a fluid pint?". After a pause from the room, we both give in.

"568ml" we both call out.

"Correct".

With that, we raise our glasses to one another.

"I should be heading back now" he says looking down.

It annoys me that I don't want this to end, but I give in and agree with him.

"Me too" I say.

"It was good to meet you" he says, turning to walk off.

"And you" I slowly walk back to my table.

We don't win the quiz. Neither does bar guys team.
It seems the locals managed to win based on entertainment

trivia questions, which there were more of, whereas our forte was the STEM topic, or literature due our very own expert, Reed.

Hey ho. The prize wasn't exactly mind blowing anyway. It consisted of some bottles of alcohol, local cheese, a free drink for each team member this evening, some vouchers, and £50 cash. Which let's face it wouldn't have been so useful between us all.

"Whose Mr know it all?" Drew asks me.

"Huh?" is all I can muster up.

"The guy stood at the bar with you earlier".

"Oh. Not a clue. Just a fellow nerd I suppose".

"Well, he's been looking at you for most of the night. You either have an extremely nice neck, or his eyes are made of iron and you're a magnet".
Nice little throwback to the quiz question Drew.

"I vote on the magnet" – Thanks Si. *Not.* He's such a Slytherin; Ambitiously leading the debate with his opinions. Sure to be followed by his minions. Not that Slytherins are bad. He's pretty cool *most of the time*. Just a tad infuriating.

"Me too" – Always a sheep, never a wolf, Pip.
Ugh.

"yep" – Drew started this and still has to have a dig. Douchebag.

"Agreed" – To round it off, thank you Reed. All four of them agree.
I thought you were better than that Reed.

"Are you saying I don't have a sexy neck?" I say, disgusted in the lack of support from these noobs I call friends.

"No comment" Drew says.
The others all look away.
I decide not to continue with the conversation.
I'm the youngest, yet most mature. Clearly. I think as I huff and cross my arms like a child who can't get their own way.

Since I'm sat with my back to Mr bar guys table, I have no excuse to look over, which has quite frankly saved me. The urge to peak at him has been present. I won't lie.

Perhaps being deep in work over the last few years has numbed my mind and body to the idea of having some romantic company in my life.

I mean, I have enough company with the four I'm sitting at this table with, not to mention Oli; the sixth friend in our group, back at home, and Flic; the seventh friend and only other female. So, there hasn't been space in this overworking brain to consider dating or enjoying another person's company… until him. I have had a few non-serious relationships. When I say a few, I quite literally mean two. And no. I'm not classing the boyfriend I had pre-amputation from year four, who I kissed twice and held hands with every day until he dumped me for a piece of chewing gum. That's how much I'm worth apparently.

I'm never usually the type to just focus on looks, but it's safe to say now that I've shared a few quiz questions and answers, found some common ground and spoke to him without making an idiot of myself (*I hope*), I'm allowed to appreciate his appearance; A delicious appearance at that.

His brown jumper looks so cosy, I want to snuggle into it. He's well-groomed but still a little…rustic.

I mean, he could be an absolute degrading, selfish, player, asshat for all I know, but I'm allowed to dream aren't I? Those intense yet soothing eyes… Deep Forest green with a dark brown outer ring. Specks of sage green in his left eye. Don't even ask how I've grasped this from the short amount of time spent with him. I'm perceptive, ok?

He's larger than me. Broader and taller. Not that it takes much. I'm just a speck of a human really. He looks like he could pick me up in one swoop, which sounds divine.
OK enough now Lista.

I order myself to cease thoughts regarding this delicious man and return to reality to play the game of cards that Pip just drew.

Chapter 2

Quin
Playlist: *Sparks Fly (Taylors Version)* – Taylor Swift

"I'm just going to go and take this call guys" I say to my group at the table, as I put on my coat and scarf.
Outside is freezing, frosty and covered in snow. Idyllic really for a Winter holiday away. There's a fire outside and a table with packs of marshmallows. How romantic.
I feel like I'm in The Holiday. The question is, would I be Jack Black, or Jude Law… Glad to be thinking of this internally rather than out loud. *Great movie.* Not that my friends would agree.

I walk to the far left, out the way of the locals' loud and cheery chatter. A quick call to my family goes well.
I take in the view of the hills and trees covered in a white blanket of snow and take a moment to myself to inhale the cold air into my lungs. It's nice. It's even nicer when I head back to the pub doors and stop to the sound of a woman's voice. It's her, from the bar. She's sat beside the fire alone on a high-backed cushioned rattan chair, that almost swallows her up. She looks so cosy. I kind of wish I was that chair. A beautiful woman in my lap. Wouldn't be half bad, would it?

"Hey bar guy. How do you feel about being defeated by the locals?" she says. I turn towards her.

Love, In Balance

"My team were gutted. But then again, I blame those trivia questions" I say, smiling.

I walk towards the chair next to hers, only separated by a small table and gesture towards it.

"Chair taken?".

"Nope, feel free" she says, smiling enthusiastically.

"What's that you're drinking" I say. She looks so content, wrapped in a deep red cardigan and scarf, holding a large mug topped with a tower of whipped cream. She smiles.

"Hot chocolate with a dash of spiced rum. Keeps me warm" she says. "What's your tipple?".

"Just a simple old fashioned to do the same thing" I say with a smile. "Cheers". I raise my glass to meet hers.

"I love a good old fashioned. I just thought I'd up the cliché cosy girl look, you know?" she says as she snuggles her hot chocolate near her face.

"Well, you're doing a good job" I respond. She smiles and her face lights up when I ask, "Are you getting any marshmallows".

"Yeah, I was just waiting for someone else to get one, so I look less desperate". She laughs and looks down, embarrassed. That was my cue. I get up and grab two skewers and two marshmallows. Luckily enough the brand is one I know, so no need to be awkward about finding vegan ones.

Despite being vegetarian and vegan my whole life, I still find it awkward to bring up in certain situations.
You know those people who love to cause a scene by questioning your diet choices? Yeah. I like to avoid that as much as possible. Otherwise I just feel like punching someone in the nose for prying for no good reason.

"Well, I'm grabbing one, so, care to join?". Her eyes brighten at my invitation. She puts her mug down and leaps up to grab one from me.

"Don't mind if I do!" she says enthusiastically.
We toast our marshmallows successfully and take our seats again.

"So, how cheated do you feel in regard to the quiz?" she asks. I grasp my chest, faking heartbreak before being serious again.

"I mean, we clearly raised the bar in the academia section, but sadly entertainment trivia just takes over every time" I respond with shrugged shoulders and take a bite of my toasted marshmallow, letting her fill the silence.

"I know. It's not my strong section, clearly. If it included questions about romance novels, horror movies, games and animals, I'd have more of a chance" she says, laughing into her hot chocolate.

"Same but replacing the romance novels with academic texts and comics. Also, I think we're perhaps a few decades too young for many of the questions. So, they had the upper hand" I say, nervous about assuming her age, but she laughs, nonetheless.

"Very true. I'm not too bothered though. The locals will cherish the winner's prize more than we would" she says through a mouthful of marshmallow. I nod in agreement, smiling and sipping my drink.

Even with so many woolly layers on, and her mouth stuffed with marshmallow, she's genuinely gorgeous. My mind starts wishing it was something else stuffing her mouth, but I'm quick to halt those thoughts.

I'm trying not to stare, but this view is too good to miss. She's smiling into her hot chocolate, the light from the fire illuminating her face. Her hair, up in a messy bun with bangs hanging loosely either side of her face. Little whisps sticking out, the fire reflecting on them. She looks ethereal.

I look down at her legs and notice how one of them sits differently through her tights and the colour is just slightly darker than her skin below the knee. I'm almost certain her leg is prosthetic below the knee, and I am in awe.

Her ocean eyes look towards me, catching me watching her. Her smile widens and my embarrassment causes me to laugh under my breath and look down at my drink. She decides to respond to my gazing.

"It's totally fine to look at my leg. I'm used to it. She usually gets all of the attention anyway" she says, referring to her prosthetic and gives me a wink.

Her honesty and upfront manner are refreshing. It makes me admire her even more.

This is so unlike me. I never really notice women, let alone set my focus on them. There's just something different about her in my eyes.

I feel a pull to her, although I'm not one to believe in *love at first sight.*

She sips her drink and gets whipped cream on her nose. She laughs and wipes it off.

"It's nice to speak to someone different tonight. I've spent the week with those lot so it's nice to have a fresh conversation with a cool like-minded individual" she says. Thank goodness she didn't find me creepy looking at her like that.

Sort yourself out Quin.

"It's nice to speak to you too. Honestly that's the first time someone's described me as cool though. I'm not so sure" I say with a low laugh.

"Oh, come on. You're clearly intellectual, funny and charming. Don't sell yourself short" she says to me.

To me.

"Charming ay? Well, people at work probably wouldn't agree. And I'm sure my mates would take the piss. You're cool too" *And stunning.* "I haven't met many people who could even attempt to answer those academic questions, so it was awesome to see" I say.

"Well, thank you. Likewise. Same wavelength". We both smile and hold each other's gaze shortly. Her eyes taking breaks, looking around but always coming back to me, before we get pulled out of the moment by an interruption I do *not* appreciate.

"Quin, are you coming in?". It's Edward; my best friend and colleague, summoning me.

"Yep, I'll be in soon" I say to him whilst side eyeing that I'm currently occupied.

"Sorry I didn't realise he had company" Edward says to... I didn't ask her name. *Shit.* I'm sure her friend called her Lista or something along those lines earlier.

"We met at the bar earlier during the quiz. We Just bumped into one another again. This is... Lista?" I half say and half ask. "I believe I heard correctly earlier".
She smiles at me.
"You are correct. I'm not sure how we've been speaking all this time and not asked each other's names" she says. "I'm guessing yours is Quin?".
Hearing my name from her mouth is addictive.

"Yep" I say, just smiling back. I think I've smiled more this evening than I have this entire year. My cheeks hurt. What has gotten into me?
"This is Edward. My best mate".

"Good to meet you Edward" she says, politely.

"You too Lista. Nice work at the quiz! Those locals totally busted our balls" he replies to her, awkwardly, realising he's disrupted our conversation.

"Tell me about it! Anyway, Quin, Edward, I'm going to head in before the guys think I've been kidnapped. Although a break from them is always welcomed. Maybe I'll see you before the night ends" she says with a smile as she looks straight at me. She walks into the pub leaving Edward and I alone.

"Well, that's a shock. Quin Russell talking to a woman…" Edward says.

I walk off before I can be interrogated by him.

After a few hours, the pub owners usher everyone outside for the New Year's countdown. There's a large inviting box with 'sparklers' written on the front, and two men setting up fireworks a little further down in the space the pub owns. After a few whiskeys and the guys feeling merry too, I'm feeling rather…unlike myself. I feel warm and fuzzy.

Shit, maybe I am the Jude Law type. No crying Quin. I search the crowd of people gathered outside the pub, looking for Lista. I really hope she hasn't left. Not that it matters after tonight anyway I guess.

I feel a bump on my back and turn to nudge Edward, but when I look round, I see a petite, gorgeous girl looking up at me with those stormy ocean eyes. Very grateful I didn't decide to elbow who I thought was Edward.

"Lista".

"Hey Quin. I happened to see you so thought I'd stand around here for the countdown. Plus, I got us both sparklers to pay you back for the marshmallows". She has a mischievous, half embarrassed expression as she bites back a smile and hands me a sparkler. I nudge her arm with mine slightly and face towards where the fireworks are being lit.

Love, In Balance

Both of us smile.

"10…9…8…7…" You know the rest.

I don't know what comes over me, but when everyone shouts, "Happy New Year!", Lista and I seem to be facing each other, smiling. I learn forward towards her, not sure if we're about to hug. I take her waist. She lifts her hands around my shoulders and links her fingers behind my head… and our lips meet. We kiss.

Her lips are warm and soft, a contrast to the crisp freezing air surrounding us. It feels like a welcome home kiss. The best kiss of my life, and yet it's so brief.

I still feel it when we pull away from each other. Her eyes beautiful. Her smile wide, and her cheeks pink.

The fuzzy feeling in my body is something I've never felt before. She takes a piece of paper out of her pocket and puts it into my hand. I smile. She tip-toes up to meet my ear.

"My phone number is on that paper. Text me if you like, but no pressure. Thank you for a great evening" She whispers, following it with a kiss to my neck.

I get shivers down my spine.

Little does she know.

She pulls away to look at me. I open her hands and place a piece of paper in hers. I lean down towards her, kiss her neck and whisper "Same wavelength".

Chapter 3

Lista

Playlist: *Down bad* – Taylor swift

It's been two weeks, and I'm still wishing I was back in The Lake District. The crunch of snow beneath my feet. The crisp air kissing the skin on my face.

And other things I'd rather not think too deeply about since I've been led on just to be let down *again*.

I've clearly been ghosted. *Again.* It fucking sucks.

I can't say I expected him to actually show interest in me romantically, or even at all for that matter.
I'm the friend who's always second best.

Always the bridesmaid, never the bride is the phrase, if I'm correct.

I'm the short, nerdy one who hangs around with guys. I'm not exactly the conventionally beautiful type that people fantasize about.

Plus, I'm pretty sure he paid some attention to my leg, which is often the deal breaker for potential romance.

My leg is well and truly my personal cock block. *Thanks a lot leg. No, I'm just kidding, you're perfect.* And believe me, it doesn't impact my…bedroom abilities. *Wink wink.*

Love, In Balance

I spend most of my days studying and working. Doing a full-time PhD is anything but glamorous.

I'm on campus most of the week surrounded by dudes, and my main fashion staple is dungarees and doc martens.

The only time I escape the norm is when I'm working as a lived experience practitioner across various departments. So, I'm a student and an associate with the uni.

Odd to be honest, but it keeps me on my toes (real and prosthetic). And keeps my pockets lined.

I may as well live here. I can't complain though. The consistency keeps me from having to deal with too much change and travel.

I struggle in those aspects, so being in one place helps.

My other venture is my part time freelance mechanical engineer job, and currently I'm doing a biomechanical research project, so I'm getting as much experience as possible by looking for bioengineers to shadow, particularly those working in the development of prosthetics.

I may have even pestered my prosthetist enough for him to let me shadow him every once in a while.

You're probably thinking, Lista how do you juggle it all? The answer is, I have no choice. I own my own apartment, alone, and have done since I left the care system at seventeen, so the bills need paying. Simple. My aunt does still help me when I need an extra pair of hands, or legs, but after what life has thrown at me, I like to prove to myself I can be independent and reliable. So I like working hard.

That's *my* life, and I'm happy. Most of the time.

Today is a slow and flexible day.

I'm working on research, whilst also taking some time out to do some individual work.

The first on my list is a quick session with a masters nursing group. I'm scheduled to discuss my experience in A&E as a person with mental health difficulties, plus how my physical difficulties are treated due to being an amputee and having lasting effects from a head injury.

I've had tonnes of experience, from the moment I was rushed into accident and emergency after the accident, to right now. A whole fifteen years of hospital visits to look back on. It's a draining session but extremely rewarding and makes me hope that I can help make the next generation of nurses even better. I'm then finishing off my day by sitting in on a biomechanical engineering seminar.

I decided to do my solo research in this field due to my interests in the particular branch of engineering, plus for future career prospects too, so I'm looking forward to it. It should be insightful, but a nice, easy going way to end my day.

I head over to the coffee shop on campus and fetch a chamomile tea to ease my nerves and ground me, and a vegan sausage roll to tame the beast growling within my stomach. I spend my break sitting in the cosiest corner of the library, like the true introvert I am, and enjoy some headspace.

I head up to the masters nursing classroom and settle in before discussing my experiences.

The turnout is good, and the Q&A session goes extremely well. I discuss the lack of space in the A&E waiting area for those with mental health struggles, and how the staff treated me too. The biggest chunk of the story I wanted the students to take away from my talk was how I was disregarded by A&E nurses and doctors after going to be seen about extreme headaches and fatigue.

Due to my past, they shrugged it off as being connected to my head injury and assumed it was a symptom with a clear source and explanation. It took all my strength and pleading for them to take more tests, to which they were proved wrong. It had nothing to do with my head injury and everything to do with my extreme iron deficiency, that wouldn't have been picked up if I'd allowed them to just discharge me based on their assumptions. These stories *need* to be told and more importantly, listened to, in order to make students into better practitioners upon moving into their careers.

I give my positive and negative experiences and also tips on how things could be better in these environments that clearly are not designed for neurodivergent and mentally ill people like me. I hope to make a difference in small doses. I get some great feedback and seem to motivate the students. So as far as this work goes, I'm pleased.

Sometimes I mess up, trip over my words or get so anxious that I have to contact the team and cancel, but today was a good day. I'm proud of those little achievements.

Whilst I was delivering my discussion, I noticed a tall figure walk past the narrow window of the door, in the hallway. I only saw his face very briefly.

Dark hair ruffled slightly but combed into a smart look. Dark eyes slightly concealed by glasses, and dressed immaculately in a crisp white shirt, only the collar sticking

out from a deep brown cosy jumper. Why did he seem so familiar from just a short glance?
He kind of looked like Quin, the bar guy, but I know I'm now being ridiculous. *Wishful thinking.*
I dismiss these thoughts as I walk through the hallways to my next session.

Going from a member of staff to a regular student, I take a seat closest to the wall in the seminar room, out of the way of everyone else since I'm not officially part of this class. But then again, I'd do this anyway.
I must say, I'm serious about my job as a professional introvert. I keep my head down, arranging my notebook, pens and highlighters, research questions, and drink.

After keeping my mind occupied and my head down whilst everyone else piles into the room and takes their seats, I look up to spot the man I saw during my discussion earlier. He's the other side of the room so the distance between us is enough to blur the definitions of his face without my glasses on, but when he looks up and straight towards me, I realise exactly who it is.

It's Quin. The bar guy from New Year's Eve, who kissed me passionately and then ghosted me.
I wasn't imagining things. It's definitely him.
Great. Wonderful. Spiffing! Fucking brilliant.
That must be why we both recognised one another when we first met. We must have seen each other in the halls.
Plus, I've only just started sitting in on the bioengineering classes, so perhaps our paths wouldn't have crossed prior. Maybe he's new.
Ugh I don't know!

Love, In Balance

He looks at me for a few seconds before it becomes evident that he has also realised who I am. His eyes widen, and he tilts his delicious lips into a one-sided smile before looking away. Despite how difficult it is to stop the muscles in my face from reacting to him, I *do not* smile back.

So, not only do I feel like absolute shit from being ghosted, but I now have to share this entire seminar in the same room as said ghost-er (*ghost? I don't know what you call it*) and go on with my life knowing he attends the same university as me.

I'm just glad he isn't on my course, or else I guess I'd have to up and move far away. Ok now I'm just being irrational. I do my best to completely avoid him during the session. Eyes on the professor and the lesson. Staying sharp. I think my lack of luck has peeked, until halfway through the seminar the professor introduces the next tutor.

You guessed it. It's Quin *fucking* Russell.
Probably his actual middle name.

So now my lack of luck has peeked for sure. He's not a student. He's a tutor…I kissed a tutor.
I mean, kind of hot, but also kind of *ew*.
I thought he was the same age as me, but now that I think about it, he must be closer to Drew and the guys in age, which isn't *that* bad. It could be so, so much worse. Plus, I'm of legal age. It's not like I'm a child who kissed a middle-aged professor. *Ok that made me feel a little sick.* My mind is spiralling.

I can see he is trying to remain professional. He's doing a good job. Other than fidgeting with his hand, which currently has a support strap on it. I'm not entirely bitter. I can appreciate a good lecturer.

A fellow academic who has clearly worked his way up to this point. I know how hard the guys worked to get to there so I can't deny the respect I have for him.

He does hold his gaze on me every so often whilst the other tutor speaks, and despite the guilt in his eyes when he finds mine, the rest of the time he's direct, to the point and confident. I see how he could be mistaken for a dick. No messing around or tolerating shitty behaviour from people. Just pure, serious teaching. He embodies none of the traits I saw when we first met on New Year's Eve. He's strait-laced and strict. Happily calling people out on their disrespectful behaviour.

It earns him some huffs and sighs, but I'm in full support of his style of teaching. I've had to put up with this shit from students whilst doing my lived experience work, and the tutors I work with just allow it, so it's refreshing to see his response to those in his class.

A student decided to have his phone out, whilst clearly not paying attention, and Quins response was to sit on his desk in silence until the guy looked up from his screen, realising no further teaching was taking place after a few moments.

"Everything ok there Jason?" he asks the student, who replies with a nod and quiet "yeah".
Quin stands up and paces the front of the room.

"Now, this goes for everyone. If my lecture isn't up your street, feel free to leave. I'm aware people have urgent messages, but I feel like some of your phones may have held your attention much longer than I have during this lesson. And it's become a habit too over the last week. If you want to be here, pay attention. If not, be my guest and leave" he says, gesturing to the door. Not with a raised voice or harsh tones, just in a matter-of-fact way, before returning to the lesson as if nothing happened.

Why am I turned on by that?

His deep, smooth voice is perfectly articulate. His clothes are a perfect mix of nerdy, professional and casual all at once, somehow. The way he sweeps back his hair every so often is enticing. And when he licks his lips, I can almost remember how they tasted. But then I remember that I'm me. It was clearly a mistake on his part to kiss me that night, hence why he stopped replying to me.
I was a mere pit stop, like I always seem to be. The drunken mistake, perhaps.

My self-consciousness creeps in and I wish I could just disappear. Surrounded by a room full of attractive, intelligent students, I stick out horribly, as always. A nerdy, petite, mud-haired, dull eyed, lame mess. How did I ever think there could have been something between us that night. Why would someone like him, be interested in someone like me? I ruminate unhealthily, and I feel myself spiralling into dangerous, unkind mental territory.
Thanks imposter syndrome. Big thumbs up for your support.

The seminar finishes and it's time for the university to close, thankfully. I can go home and attempt to remove this negative train of thought brought on by my good friend Body dysmorphia and her roomie Imposter syndrome.
I can already visualise the hot bath full of gloriously scented bubbles, followed by some tasty food and cuddles with my snuggle buddy kitty, Edith. She listens to my problems and offers the occasional comforting '*meow*'.

She always knows what to say to make things better.

Drew or Flic usually help me stop these kinds of self-deprecating tangents, but right now I'm too embarrassed to admit that the guy who ghosted me is a lecturer in a class that I need to sit in often for my research proposal.

Plus, Drew took off early to spend the day helping Flic with some DIY furniture, so I'm not willing to disturb *both* of them. Plus I can feel something on the horizon with those two, and I will not be the one to interrupt that.

So, as I do most of the time, I'm going to internalise my struggles and drown my sorrows in my evening of bliss.

It's always been important for me to have a crisis plan, to find ways to help myself when my mind starts to struggle, or I lose control. I've come so far, so I don't let things take my strength away too easily. This is certainly not going to.

I'll let myself feel and then close the door behind the bad thoughts and feelings on their way out.

I'm always the last to leave my classes.

It comes down to being terrified of holding others up by losing balance, tripping or causing an obstacle, so I find it easier to leave last, when I know I can't be a hindrance to anyone or accidently trip them up with my cane.

Except today it serves me the pain of remaining in here, with him for longer than necessary.

He and I are the last to leave, but before I can scurry out of the door, a firm grasp on my left hand makes me jolt back and stop.

I turn around to him towering over me, far too close. I step back and look up.

How is he even more attractive than the last time I saw him? His glasses are the perfect fit for his face and add that extra ounce of nerdiness. He didn't have them on when we first met, but wow they have a mighty impact. His square jaw is kissed with light stubble. His eyes are hopeful yet pleading as he stares into me.

He's also wearing the same coat he wore on New Year's Eve. His familiar smoky, yet fresh scent fills my mind with memories of him holding me. How wonderful of me to find myself in this situation.

This should be fun.

Chapter 4

Quin

Playlist: *Start Over* – Imagine dragons

I knew the moment I stood briefly outside of that classroom that it was her.

The woman I kissed on New Year's Eve, as fireworks lit up the sky. The petite, gorgeous, intelligent woman I haven't stopped thinking about since.

I thought she was a tutor, but after seeing her in my biomechanical seminar, I'm not so sure.

She was lecturing the nursing class I walked by earlier, but now she's sat taking notes in my class. This makes my thoughts about her seem wrong.

Fuck. She's upset. I can see that, but I need a chance to explain why I didn't text her back.
Whether she'll believe me or not.

She's even more stunning than I remember.

Her dark hair, long and tucked behind her ears. Bangs hanging loosely around her face.
I tried to keep it together during the seminar, but every time my eyes found her, I felt her lips on mine again.
And now I'm staring at them. Those fucking delightful lips that were set on mine. The warmth, spice and sweetness of her tongue entwining with mine. She's somehow left a

lasting impression on my barely touched soul.

I've thought about her when I've been alone over the last few weeks. I've thought some… inappropriate things. I now have no idea how old she is, and I'm scared to find out. I pulled her away from the door so we could speak before we left the site, but she does not look like she wants to discuss matters right now. I guess I can't blame her for that. Most would do the same.

She moves back from me, which pains me slightly, and she seems to take me in for a moment. I do the same before breaking the silence.

"Lista I can explain…" She cuts me short before I can continue.

"Quin, whilst I'd love to chat any other time, I'd rather not do this. I don't need to hear your excuses, ok? You don't owe me anything. I'm just a random girl you happened upon. I just need to be home right now so I can pretend today never happened".

"Please Lista, hear me out" I say tapping her shoulder, almost begging her not to leave. She turns back to me fiercely. I'm slightly nervous I might get my nose broken too if I continue.

"Look Quin, I'm fucking embarrassed and humiliated enough as it is, so please just give me the benefit of the doubt and let me walk away. This is weird enough as it is".

As she goes to turn away again, I have to just say it, so she knows I'm not a complete douche.

"Lista, I lost my phone. It wasn't my choice not to message you back" I say desperately hoping she won't just dismiss me. She turns back around, lips turned into a sarcastic smile and shaking her head lightly.

"Are you serious? You don't need to make me feel better about ghosting me by making up some stupid excuse now that you're forced to see me Quin. I get it. I'm fucking used to guys doing this, so spare me the shit".

"Lista, I swear. Please. I might be a grumpy asshole according to my students, but I'm not a liar. I wouldn't do that to someone. You can ask Edward. He was there when it happened".

She places her bag down and sits on the nearest surface, which happens to be my class desk. It's not the right time, but she looks so good sat there right now.
 I imagine pulling her legs apart and standing right there in the middle of them, feeling her warmth against me and breathing in her sweet scent.

"Ok. I'm listening. What happened?".
Thankfully she's letting me explain, whilst also pulling my thoughts back into acceptable territory.

"Edward and I had just made it back home on New Year's Day. After I replied to your first text, I didn't want to come across as too eager, so I didn't plan on texting back straight away. I'm aware that sounds fucking stupid, but I'm not all that experienced at this" I say, sighing. "Before I had the chance to finally message, whilst we were out, we were jumped by a group of guys. We fought as much as we could" I hold the hand with the support strap up "but they ended up with my phone and Edwards wallet. Police are still trying to track them down but no luck as of yet".

She sighs, closing her eyes.
 "So, you didn't purposely ghost me?" she asks.

 "Why would I do that Lista? I wouldn't have given you my number just to do that."

 "Well, I'm used to shit like this happening with guys so…"

 "Look I'm sorry" I say, perhaps more forcefully than I anticipate.

 "You know what Quin, It's ok. If what you're saying is true then I've been beating myself up over nothing, which is annoying but kind of nice. I hope you and Edward are ok by the way" she says kindly but withdrawn.

 "What do you mean beating yourself up? I'm the one who fucked up".

 "Well, beating myself up for expecting *anything*. Blaming myself for…being *me*. I thought if it were anyone else. Any other beautiful woman who happened to kiss you, that you'd have been in touch. If I didn't have *differences* to my body… But it doesn't matter Quin. Thanks for letting me know. Now we can resume our lives, extremely awkwardly for a while knowing that our paths will continue to cross".

"Lista, what you're saying isn't true. I genuinely wanted to message you more than anything. I spent days gutted that I had no way of contacting you. I never thought I'd see you again–".

"Until now". She finishes my sentence.

We gaze at one another in silence for a few seconds before the professor co-lecturing my class earlier suddenly barges in.

"Oh sorry, I just forgot my folder".

I have to make this situation seem normal, so I say the first thing that comes to mind.

"It's ok. I was just discussing something with this student. We're leaving now". I give Lista an apologetic look. She gets up and walks away out the doors as I finish my sentence holding her gaze.

"Thanks Quin".

"Bye Lista". She leaves, and I feel like the biggest arsehole.

Love, In Balance

"So, I see you've met Callista. She's a bright student and associate here with the university. She's not part of this class but she's joining us every so often to gain more insight for her research proposal, hence her appearance here today".

"Right, thanks. I didn't realise her full name was Callista. Would you be able to send me her email please, so I can become acquainted with her, should she need any information for future sessions". *And maybe so I can message her and apologise even further for being the cause of her sadness.* After previous happenings, I try my best to conceal what we were discussing and act as though what he walked in on was just a student and tutor, talking about... educational stuff, as opposed to the whole kissing and accidental ghosting situation.
The latter probably wouldn't have gone down so well.

"Yes, do you have a pen to hand?" he says.

I write down her email and feel a spark inside knowing I can contact her. I can't bear to leave it like this between us.
 I might be withdrawn and supposedly grumpy during my work hours, but I'm not a dick, especially not to someone like Lista.
 I rub my thumb over the email I have written down, 'Callista.Harper97@hotmail.co.uk'. What a beautiful name.

I head home and instantly set open my laptop.
My cat Edison hops onto my lap for a cuddle, but I can't help the need to send this email as quickly as possible. My mind is spiralling. Trying to convince me that if I wait another minute, the chance will be gone to make further amends with Lista. I do not feel as close to being forgiven as I'd personally like, so this is something I need to do.

Whilst manoeuvring my arms around my little fluff ball Edison, who may as well be attached to me upon getting home from work, I manage to write out an email.

To: *Callista.Harper97@hotmail.co.uk*
Subject: *Please read.*

Callista,
It's Quin Russell. This is my personal email since this is a matter beyond work.
I didn't want to just leave the way our conversation ended earlier. I got your email from Professor Peters, so I hope you don't mind me reaching out.
I'm just sorry for everything. What I said was the truth. I may be strict on campus, but in my personal life I'm not a dick. I don't treat people like they're disposable. I'm sorry I made you feel that way. It had nothing to do with you, just a shitty situation I couldn't fix, so I'm sorry you felt so awful. I wish I could do it all over again and not lose the piece of paper you gave me.
I hope you can forgive my shitty actions. I'd really appreciate us talking in person again to not leave on such a shit note.

Love, In Balance

My mum always says, 'Never leave on an argument' and my track record is perfect. I can't break that now.

Best wishes,

Quin Russell

I re-read it about ten times. I even ask Edison what he thinks, but he's very conveniently fallen asleep in my lap. I click send and hope it's good enough for Lista. Even the cliché part about my mums saying may have taken it a little too far. Joking after what must be a shitty day for her might not have been my best move. She deserves my sincerest apologies. Hearing her talk about being used to being ghosted and beating herself up about me not messaging her back made me feel fucking angry. I want to fuck over anyone who has made her feel unworthy and understand why.
Why has she been treated like this before?
Why is she believing herself to be unworthy?
And why would she blame herself for letting this happen?
  She is literally the most gorgeous human I've come across, and the way she makes me feel when I'm near her is dangerous. Every day away from her since we kissed feels like a loss. I've dreamt about her in obscene ways and today seeing her again resurfaced those tenfold. She may not wanting anything more from me after what's happened, but I'd rather risk my feelings and make amends than have her feel unworthy.

Chapter 5

Lista
Playlist: *Figure it out* – Royal Blood

On my way out of campus I bumped into a familiar face. Not one I expected to see after the monstrosity of the day's events already, but it put things into place for me thankfully. And now my busy brain can take one overthinking job off of its to-do list.

"Lista… I did not expect to see you here! It's Edward, from New Year's Eve. Do you work here?". *As if. Small world.*

"Oh, hi Edward. Yes, I remember you. Good to see you". I struggle to know what to say. I'm still slightly shaking and overwhelmed from speaking to Quin. "I'm actually a PhD engineering student and an associate too during my spare time".

"Oh, ok. Well, what a small world.". *Tell me about it…* "I'm a tutor here. Although you probably guessed that" he says whilst gesturing to the open classroom door that he's manning. "I honestly didn't think I'd see or hear from you again after what happened. Quin hasn't stopped going on about you since we got home. He was like a lost puppy". *This makes me feel all tingly inside.* "And after having our things stolen, things have been... difficult. Of course, he lost his phone and couldn't message you, so he's been giving himself a pretty hard time. I mean, he had to go to hospital for his injuries, yet all he gave a shit about was not being able to text you back".

"Wait, so you guys were actually robbed?" He looks at me confused by what I've just asked. Probably also wondering why it's the only part of this discussion I've decided to respond to.

"Well yeah. Have you seen Quin? If so, did he not mention it? I thought it'd be obvious by his limp and arm. Not to mention his fucking ribs. They're pretty badly bruised. He broke a couple of them" he says, whilst almost wincing, followed by a look down, almost filled with shame. "He took the brunt unfortunately. If it wasn't for him, I'd have been screwed. I got away with a few minor scratches and bruises, whilst that poor bastard is broken and bent by playing the hero".

He looks down awkwardly and lifts his hand to scratch the back of his head, clearly having triggered some feelings from the incident that happened. I don't want to pry or bring up any tough memories any further. Plus I'm a little lost for words for once. I feel like the worst of humanity. The way I treated Quin, after everything he's been through. I need to go home and face plant my floor.

"I really hope you're both ok Edward. I'm glad that you guys are safe over all else. It's nice to see you… but I need to head off. I'll probably see you around" I say as I swiftly walk off to my car and head home. I feel awful leaving him so suddenly after he just slightly poured the contents of his guilt out to me. But there is something more important I need to do right now.

It's 5pm. I'm home and ready to wind down, but nothing will stop me from feeling like the biggest dickhead worldwide for how I spoke to Quin.
I should've given him more of a chance and realised that not everyone is a prick. *Well*, most people are, in my experience, but there are a few who restore my faith in humanity.
Maybe Quin could be one of them.
I need to see him and rectify this.
With karma and all that shit, I need to be in the universes good books. I've been a good person all these years, despite the trauma and loss I've faced, and I'm not letting *this* make me break my good streak. Karma is not making me her bitch over a misunderstanding with a guy. *Nope*. Not on my watch.

After speaking to Edward, it's clear that Quin was actually telling me the truth. What are the odds?!
Either that, or him and Edward are extremely good at acting. Or perhaps it's some sort of folie à deux.
I open my laptop to find a few email notifications.

I read the first one in my inbox and my heart aches. It's from Quin. I immediately reply.

To: Russell.Quin90@hotmail.com
Re: Please read

Quin,

Thanks so much for emailing, I really appreciate it. I'll be at Cosy Corner Coffee tonight from 6pm. We can chat in person if you come along. I'd love a chance to prove I'm a better human being than I've let on so far.

Your mum sounds wise. Never leave on an argument.

Hopefully see you soon.

Callista Harper MSc
PhD mechanical engineering student
Lived experience practitioner

I walk into Cosy Corner Coffee, where I always get my cosy drink fix, at 6pm. I decided to come here to make an excuse for Quin to see me after our misunderstanding today. Not that I expect him to meet me with such short notice. *Again*, wishful thinking.

After waving to Lilah, the coffee shops incredible, not to mention, gorgeous owner, I walk to my usual spot at the back, tucked away nicely, because that's the kind of introvert I am. This place is rustic, simple and cosy, which basically describes Cosy Corner Coffee up perfectly.

It's my favourite place to be. Lilah offered me a wink and pointed discretely towards my usual little nook.
I was confused momentarily until I approach my seat; A set of two comfortable armchairs surrounding a small oak coffee table, positioned in front of a bookshelf.
One chair occupied by Quin.
I actually cannot believe it. He's actually here. Plus, he's sat at my favourite table, as if he knew. He stands and looks at me, hands in his pockets with a sorry smile on his face.

"Thank you for giving me a chance to talk in person again, away from campus. I hope this seat's ok". He looks insanely gorgeous in the warm light of the late-night coffee shop. I'm surrounded by my favourite smells and now get to experience that whilst looking at a new favourite sight.

I walk towards him and close the distance between us. He's standing tall and broad, with a confident stance.

"No, thank *you* for turning up, even when I spoke to you like shit earlier. I'm really sorry about that. It's just a response to protect myself. I'm just so glad you decided to turn up. I didn't expect you to" I sigh "Oh, and this is the best seat in the house. It's my favourite spot" I say with a smile, trying to brighten up my tone. "You chose well".
I've had enough of feeling shitty. It's good for no one.

"Well, things aside, let's sit down and get comfortable" he says, smoothing his hand down my arm towards the chair. "I got us both drinks, but if you aren't feeling it, I can get you something else. I just remembered what you were drinking on New Year's and took a chance, minus the spiced rum. I got it with oat milk too. I hope that's ok. I didn't want to take any chances with milk choice". He says scratching his head and looking to down with a brief hushed laugh.

My insides are melting at how sweet that is. He bought me a drink, remembered what I was drinking last time, and managed to make it vegan without even knowing.

"You really did not have to do that. I should be the one trying to win *you* over… but thank you so much. It's perfect. I'm vegan, so oat milk was a good call". His confident smile grows wider and his eyebrow lifts.

"Snap" he says.

He's vegan too. Why do I now feel *even more* attracted to him?

The conversation flows and has these lovely comfortable silences that make me feel safe and content.

We really do just seem to get on well, despite the hiccup of our earlier run in. It really was all just one big misunderstanding. He tells me exactly what had happened the day he and Edward were robbed. I demand he show me his arm and foot. They're badly bruised and tender due to the fractures and trauma. Apparently, most of his abdomen is similar.

I'm definitely *not* thinking about that… Well, trying not to.

I feel awful for not believing him. I've just been hurt so many times that the probability of him genuinely having a real excuse to not reply was low.

I explained this to him, and he seems to understand, thankfully. In true Callista style, I apologise at least once every fifteen minutes to him.

How do people treat others like shit and live with it?

I've been defensive in this scenario to protect myself and yet I feel so guilty for my actions. Like, losing sleep kind of guilty. He notices me ruminating and places his hand gently over mine, offering a small squeeze.

His hand engulfs mine and the warmth from him flows through my body from this small point of contact. He's sweet and lovely, but so manly it makes me quiver.

One big dichotomy, yet somehow so beautifully balanced.

"Callista, I've told you, it's ok. You've done nothing wrong. I understand why you found it hard to believe me. It's a pretty unbelievable set of circumstances. But it's in the past now".

Why is the guy who lost my number and then got beat up and robbed the only decent guy I seem to have come across? Literally everyone else ghosts me without giving a shit or tells me to my face that I'm not their type before swiftly leaving. Usually It's once they've realised I'm minus half a leg. It angers me that it makes such a difference to people's opinions of me.

"Right ok. In the past it is… I'm possibly still going to keep apologising. It's just who I am. When I do wrong, I like to make sure the person knows that It's not in me to make someone feel like shit".

"Lista, I know. I can tell you're one of the genuine ones. And I'd like to think I am too" he says with a slight sigh.

His voice is so deep and smooth. *Ugh* I want to record him reading my favourite book and play it over and over again. He's got a deep, yet smooth voice with a classy bite to his accent. He reminds me of Matthew Macfadyen's Darcy, and I'm living for it.

Love, In Balance

"So, why do people think you're a dick at the Uni?" I ask before thinking, genuinely curious. Not realising it may open up a can of worms (*I've never understood that saying*). He looks at me with a look that says "*Really?*", and his eyebrows pinch together, but he answers, nonetheless. He could quite easily shut me down and tell me to mind my own business, but he pushes through. What a saint.

"So, I take my job seriously. I've worked my way up from where my students are now. I had to gain respect from my fellow students, professors, industry professionals and basically every academic I came across for over ten years. I got kicked down, had some tough years training, and then in my first year of teaching was told that I was 'too down to earth' and that students had taken a favour to me in the wrong ways. I was supposedly too kind and soft and was pulled into the office because of what students were saying about me. Like what the fuck does all of that even mean?" He says whilst running his hands through his hair.

Yep. That can of worms has been opened. Might be too late to pop that lid back on.

He's calm, yet stern and holds himself well, despite feeling wound up over the current topic. He takes a few breaths and then continues. "Fellow professors told me I wouldn't be taken seriously. First year students *did* take advantage, spoke to me like I was one of them and didn't take deadlines or even seminars and lessons seriously. I was told that my behaviour around students was inappropriate and almost got a disciplinary Lista. Yet I'd done nothing but be myself. I've always kept professional boundaries. I've never treated my students differently and

I've tried to ignore any advances made to me. But yeah, I just snapped. So, now Instead of the soft and kind, *cool* lecturer, I'm now a dick, supposedly. I guess I prefer the latter if it helps my professional reputation. Although it doesn't seem to stop *some* students". He sits back in his chair with a sigh.

Round of applause Lista, you dick.

Way to bring up a stupid topic and make him feel shittier than you already have.

"Look I'm sorry for asking and bringing it all up. Let's just drink this delicious hot chocolate and forget about the shitty things. For the record, I think you're cool". I remember saying this to him on New Year's Eve.

He lifts his head and smiles knowingly. His eyes creasing at the corners.

I continue "And despite despising you whilst watching you teach today, I admired you. You were professional, passionate, articulate and made learning interesting and fun. Yes, you take no shit, but that's how it should be. We're all here to learn and improve, so no one should be anything but focused during class. You're a great lecturer and you should be proud of how you teach. I hope you get more respect from students. You deserve it. I say that as a fellow academic and student too. Plus, grumpy is kind of the new hot" I say, internally questioning why the fuck I would say that last part.

After my rather intense and passionate compliment about Quin, we share a silence that should be awkward, but it's just us, smiling at one another, with him eventually thanking me through a sigh of relief. We sit for a while longer before gathering our things and heading out.

Love, In Balance

"Thanks for giving me a chance to explain Lista" Quin says as we leave the coffee shop, and head into the crisp cold January air.

"Thank you for meeting me and letting me apologise too. I hope it's not awkward being around a student like this. I know we met prior to realising where we both are in life, but still", I say glancing around and snuggling my face into my scarf.

"Lista, I knew you outside of work first. Yes, I must admit, you were the last person I expected to see in the lecture theatre today, but it was a nice surprise. And I can sleep easy now knowing that the cosy, beautiful woman I met on New Year's Eve knows that she hasn't been ghosted by a douchebag".

I freeze for a moment before feeling the heat rise up my neck and onto my cheeks. I smile without even realising.

"I'm glad our paths crossed again, and that I know you're safe Quin" Is all I can say.

My eyes focus on his lips. Damn I could kiss him all over again. My body heats up in places other than my neck and cheeks.

Snap out of it Lista!

He looks down at me before gripping the side of my arm. "Oh and, your *'body differences'* make you even more beautiful, so don't ever worry about that…It makes you, you. Anyone who thinks any different of you, that's their issue, not yours." he says as he glances to my leg, before continuing "Get home safe anyway, and I'll see you around".

I smile up at him. "You shall".
I will most definitely be seeing you around.

I get home and I can't help but feel extremely twirly (in other words…horny, for those who aren't a complete weirdo like me). I have the relaxing bath that I promised myself, do my night-time prosthetic cleaning routine, eat a light dinner and read in bed for an hour or so before snuggling under my covers with my trusty sex toy sidekick. The spicy cowboy book I'm reading may have induced some fantasies that will remain in my mind and between the sheets. Elsie always knows how to create the sexiest book boyfriends. I take full advantage.

I enjoy a well-deserved release of pent-up energy and then fall into a calming sleep. Definitely not dreaming about a certain dark haired tall professor and what lies beneath those layers of clothing.

Chapter 6

Quin
Playlist: *Beyond* – Leon Bridges

It's been two days since Lista and I were reintroduced.

It started on a rather dull note, but after having a proper conversation over the nicest hot chocolate I've tasted, we managed to find common ground and get through the misunderstanding.

She's attended both of my seminars over the last two days, and I've had to stop myself from being distracted by her presence.

I've not spoken to her one to one, but I want to more than anything. I need to somehow distract myself from these thoughts. I'm a professor for fuck's sake. I need to reel it in and sort my shit out.

It's different with Lista. We met before realising about our positions, but I still can't lose my cool in front of other staff and students. Or else I'll be back to square one and could risk my entire career here at the university.

I've worked too hard to get to where I am. And I'd imagine she has too.

When classes finish for lunch, I head over to the campus coffee shop to get a top up of coffee and a bite to eat. Out of nowhere an enthusiastic voice startles me.

"Quin, how are you doing?" Oli says.

"Yep, not too bad thanks. You?" I say, probably a little too robotic sounding.

"I'm good. I was wondering if you fancied coming over to my mates for a game night tonight. You look like you need it. Maybe release some of that moody energy you're giving out and put it to good use" he says, with a low laugh.

I think it through. Who would want to invite *me* to a game night. Other than Edward, anyway.
I've known Oli now for just under a month. He's a final year PhD student and part time lecturer, so we've been working together closely on seminars.
He's been shadowing me during my lectures as well as having me as his advisor on his teaching skills.
He's a great guy. We clicked instantly.

Well, once we got over him telling me how handsome and '*do-able*' I was. He made sure I knew that if I like dudes, to keep him in mind.
Somehow I feel like it eased the tension and made us get along better and quicker. Now he's someone I genuinely look forward to seeing every day.

This might actually be a good thing for me. Being around like-minded people, doing something other than working.
I don't go out often, as my friends live in different cities, other than Edward. We do the odd catch up, holiday and game night, but other than that my social life is pretty uneventful, so I decide to go for it.

"You know what, yeah, I'll be there. Text me the time and location".

Love, In Balance

He pats me on the back.

"Glad to hear it. I've told my mates all about you and your handsome face. I've even got a single friend" he says, winking, and then continues. "I'll text you later".
He walks away, jolly as ever, whilst I'm here questioning why I agreed to go out, when I could just be home with my cat and avoid the pressures of socialising.

I'm not sure why the social gods have decided I need human interaction outside of lectures today, but after lunch professor Peters comes into my office to ask me about my advisor role.

"Quin, could you take on one more student on an advisory basis please. Do you have room in your schedule?".

"Sure, I'm happy to help. Who do you need me to work with and what on? If you can pass on their contact details, I'll reach out and plan a schedule with them", I say before even taking time to consider much. Still half mentally spiralling about Olivers invitation.

"Well, you already have their contact details. It's Callista Harper, PhD mechanical engineering student. She needs an advisor for her research and work on biomechanical engineering. Your work will require regular meetings advising her and ensuring her research project is at the level it should be. Please contact Miss Harper when convenient. And Quin, thank you for this. I know you're already taking on a lot". It's nice for someone to recognise the work I put in for once.

I nod, dismissing Professor Peters from my office, wishing I'd have known who the student was prior to agreeing to it.

Well, this is going to be interesting.

I clock out and head out of the campus building, into the car park. I'm actually looking forward to doing something different for once now that the initial panic has subsided.

Game night sounds good. A way to release some tension, occupy my mind, and think about something other than work… and a certain someone.

It's Friday too, so I'm thankful I don't have to be on campus for the next two days.

I'm getting sick of advances being made by some of the first-year undergrads.

I say first years, but the older students seem to be doing the same too, despite them knowing better.

I'm apparently grumpy, strict, expect too much and yet I'm apparently…hot. Which is exactly what almost got me into trouble last time. I'm not here to be looked at. I'm a tutor to be listened to. I'm here to teach and better the knowledge and practise of students.

The world needs professional, knowledgeable, respectful professionals and I'm here to make that happen.

It's just fucking difficult when my age and appearance seem to be playing against me. I never thought I'd dislike being in my early thirties, or being described as hot, but

this whole situation has given me good enough reason to be pissed. I'm pulled out of my thoughts by Lista. She's in the car park at the passenger side of her car putting her bag and coat inside. She has black dungarees on, with a cream-coloured top underneath, accompanied by black doc martens. Her hair is tied up in a messy bun with tendrils of dark hair falling around her neck and ears.
I feel bad for looking, but I can't help appreciating her.

That's when I notice Pierce; A tutor from my department approaching her car behind her. My body's defence mechanisms arise from nowhere suddenly. I decide against calling out Lista's name and head over to my car. My eyes never leaving her.

Pierce startles her and she looks visibly shaken. Her hand shooting to her chest.
She seems to relax slightly when she turns around. She must know him. My nerves start to dissipate but I still feel on edge for some reason.

I get into my car and sit for a moment, organising my things into the passenger seat at a leisurely pace so
I can make sure Lista leaves safely.

I'm no psychologist, but Lista looks reserved based on her body language.
Pierce seems to be closer than she'd like, and she shakes her head a lot in response to what he's saying.
I would be less concerned if this was the first time I've seen a woman in Pierces presence who appeared uncomfortable. But it's not. I have in fact witnessed Pierce seemingly causing women to feel confined and irritated on a number of occasions. She eventually walks away, around to the driver's side of her car. Pierce follows her and holds his

hands out from his sides as if asking *"why"* to her.
I kind of wish I knew how to read lips at this moment in time. It would help give this situation context.
She shakes her head, gets into her car and shuts the door before Pierce walks off.
When she drives away, I feel relief that she's away from him. There's just something off and I can't shake that feeling. But I'm pulled out of it by a text notification from my phone.

Oli: *Game night tonight at 6.30pm. I'll pick you up at 6.10pm from yours.*

Quin: *Cheers. See you later.*

I get home, take a long shower and decide to make myself look slightly more presentable for a game night with friends and less like a university professor heading to a professional conference.

I choose my baseball style T-shirt and roll up the sleeves. I ruffle my hair slightly, choose a pair of smart casual jeans and pair them with my checked black and white classic slip-on vans. I wear my usual coat. It actually reminds me of Lista, since I was wearing it the night we met.

I feel more…*me* with these types of clothes on, but sadly it's not often I find the casual opportunities to dress down for.

I pour myself a whiskey and coke, pack my drinks for this evening, feed my feline friend Edison his well overpriced cat food and sit watching game play throughs to make the time pass by and to help ground my busy mind.

Watching YouTube game playthroughs is a regular thing for me. It serves as a distraction, background noise and a form of entertainment for me during evenings after work or weekends in alone, with the exception of my cat for company.
Working in a serious environment and having to keep up my hard exterior to avoid any further issues can be draining, so it's nice to come home and watch something light and funny. It's good to let go, relax and laugh a little.

Oli: *I'm outside.*

That's my cue to stop cuddling Edison and actually leave the house to socialise with humans. *Not cats.*

We drive for about fifteen minutes before reaching Oli's friend's house. I'm hoping that I'm not being kidnapped and held for ransom by random strangers. I don't know Oli that well, so who knows what's about to happen. I may have been watching too many horror game playthroughs considering this is my train of thought.
Under the ruse of a game night could be all sorts of horrors. I suppose I'm about to find out.

I walk into a nice home. It's fresh but warming and the sound of laughter coming from further inside is inviting. The kidnapping probability has lowered in my mind substantially. Although when thinking logically, it was fairly low in the first place.

We walk through to the living room where there are five men, and a woman sat on the sofas and floor around a low coffee table. They all look up and greet me and Oli. The four men look familiar, but I'm too overstimulated to think

of where I know them from, plus I merely glanced and then studied something imaginary at my feet.
You know when you feel awkward in a new situation and have no idea where to look or what to do. *Yeah*. That.
  I notice Pierce, from earlier in the car park sitting with them. He turns his head towards me and lifts his beer, greeting me. I smile politely but internally my guard is up.

"Head into the kitchen through there". Oli says, pointing toward the door down the hall through the living room.
  "Deposit one's tipples, good sir. Oh and I think my single friend is in there" he says with a joking smile and a raised eyebrow. He is a great guy. I regret the thoughts of him luring me to my possible kidnapping and demise.
I take a sigh of relief when I head down the hallway and through the kitchen door.
I can use this time to adjust and breathe before socialising with everyone, although I'm really not in the mood for chatting with someone just because they're 'single'.
I'm happy just relaxing with friends.
I brace myself for walking into the kitchen, nervous for socialising with a random person without Oli here.
My mind is still a little cloudy from the last week of work and everything that's happened, so I'm a little tense and quite frankly not in the mood for getting to know someone new on a possible romantic level.
My relief however returns when I walk into the open, bright, airy kitchen.
  It's Lista. Oli's *single friend* is Lista.
She's standing with her back to me, checking her phone.

Love, In Balance

Her hair is down, loose long curls flowing against her back.
Dark, silky and smooth, with auburn streaks shimmering in the light. I had no idea it was this long.
She has a long-sleeved black top on with a skater skirt draping from her waist and stopping above her knees.
Her black brogues make a change to the rustic doc martens she's usually wearing, and I'm astonished at her leg. She has her bare legs exposed without tights or trousers, and I can finally see her **prosthetic** in its full glory.
It's the shape of a natural leg and is fitted below the knee. It's slightly darker than her skin and has the most incredible monochrome floral tattoo like pattern on the calf.
It's almost like her shoe is the vase and her leg has bloomed with a beautiful bouquet surrounding it.
I feel honoured to finally see her for her, without her leg concealed by clothes. She looks beautiful. Sexy, even. She's truly astonishing.

"Oh Quin. Hi!" she says as she spins around. "Sorry, I was in my own little world. Trying to self-regulate a little".

"Lista, it's… good to see you".

"Likewise. I didn't expect to see *you* here" she says.

Damn, I hope my presence isn't that bad. She must realise I was taken aback slightly.
"Shit, sorry Quin, I didn't mean it negatively. It's just such a surprise to see you. Sorry, my social battery is running low already" she says with a laugh under her breath.

"No offence taken. I just didn't want my presence to make you feel uncomfortable. I don't want to invade your personal time or space after everything that's happened".

"Oh my gosh, no, of course not. It's lovely to see you. Not lovely… in a weird way. Nice. It's great… that you're here". She puts her head in her hands and laughs. "Sorry! I'm just… yeah. Let me start again. Hi Quin, it's a pleasant surprise to see you here".
We both laugh as she reaches her hand out to me. I take it and we shake, mimicking a new introduction.
She's funny. I'm so glad she's here tonight. My nervous tension has dissipated and shifted into a new kind.

"It's a pleasant surprise to see you here too Lista. I didn't know anyone other than Oli and Pierce". She tenses up when I say Pierces name. I knew something was up earlier in the car park.

"Well, you know me". She says with a reassuring smile.
"And you kind of saw Drew, Pip, Si and Reed at the New Year's Eve Quiz, so technically you have many friends here. I mean, not that I'm assuming you class us as friends. I just wanted to make you feel comfortable. Shit, sorry I need to stop talk–". I put my hand against the side of her arm to stop her spiralling thoughts. Meanwhile realising where I recognised the four men in the living room from.

"Lista, relax. You *are* my friend. I might be a tutor but I'm also human. I met you personally prior to meeting you professionally. I'm happy to see the guys that way too. If they'll have me".

She looks towards my hand as I lightly grip her arm.

"Thanks Quin. I'm glad you're here".

The door to the kitchen opens and we step back from one another as if we've been caught doing something wrong. It's Drew.

"You ok in here guys? Quin, nice to see you my man. Really pleased you could make it" he says enthusiastically. He seems so genuine. It's nice.

"There are drinks in the fridge and cupboard, so just ask if you run out of your own and you can have some of mine. Oh, and Lista explained what happened to you and Edward. I hope you guys are ok man. It's a pleasant surprise to find out you work at the university. What are the odds of that?!" he says. I agree. What are the odds. I'd be quite interested to find out.

"Thanks Drew. That means a lot. Thanks for having me. I've only recently started full time, but it's nice to know you guys are part of the team" I say.

He lightly wraps his arm around Lista, and I wish I was the one doing that right now. He looks down at her and speaks softly. A little quieter than he was just. His demeanour has almost changed, just within mere seconds, from greeting to me, to now speaking to Lista. He seems almost mildly anxious. Again, *not* a psychologist. I could be wrong. Just an observation.

"You ok, you've been in here a while. We're ready to get games going so just come in whenever feels ok for you" he says. I wonder if they've got history.

Or if Lista isn't as single as Oli thinks.

"Drew, stop worrying about me. I'm fine. I just needed a breather before we start the games. Quin and I will be in soon. Now go back in there and sort the guys out" she says to him with a playful pinch to his arm. He smiles and leaves the kitchen.

"So, do you need a glass for your drink Quin?" she says as she slides down a glass for me anyway, not waiting for my response.

"Thank you M'lady" I reply. She laughs.

"You're welcome kind sir" she says, tipping her imaginary hat.

"Would you like a top up of your tipple?" I ask her.

"I think I need it" she says, sighing as though she's exhausted. I notice she has a prosecco glass, so I open the fridge and see a bottle. I lift it to her. She nods intensely.

"Thank you, Quin. You're a true gentleman. Unlike *some*" she says under her breath as she walks slowly out of the kitchen.

Love, In Balance

We're in the living room, halfway through the first game of blackjack. Lista has formally introduced me to those in the room that I've not met properly.

Flic, whose full name is Felicity (I've been forbidden from ever calling her by her full name) happens to be one of Lista's friend group that she bizarrely keeps referring to as *Five Mountains*. She hasn't told me the story behind the name, and I haven't thought too much into it either. It's quite catchy to be honest. She says that instead of listing everyone's name, she finds it easier to just refer to that set of people as the group name, so there you have it. I can't argue with that logic.

She briefly told me that there's clearly something more than just *friendship* going on between Drew and Flic, but neither have openly acknowledged it yet.

Why am I so relieved to know Drew and Lista aren't together? Well, to know Lista isn't with any of these great guys, to be honest.

Oli was pleased when we walked into the living room and Lista introduced me to people.

"As if you know Lista already Quin!" he says enthusiastically. "She's gorgeous isn't she?" he asks and offers Lista a wink as she flips him off openly.
I fight the urge to answer him. *Gorgeous* doesn't quite capture *how* stunning she is.

Lista's other friends are awesome, and they seem to want to protect her, which I'm fully in support of.
Oli happens to be one of Lista's group. He just couldn't make it to the New Year's Eve getaway apparently. And Flic was on call so had to stay home.

I already know Pierce. Lista made it clear that he is *not* part of their five mountains group and is just a friend they've known for years from the university. His character is...questionable. He works at the University as a guest lecturer, like I was before going full-time.

There's just something about him. He's sly and less genuine than the others here. I'm unsure of where he fits into things with them. Then again, maybe I'm the same. Just an odd one out.

I'm glad I have my drink in my hand because if I didn't, I'd be close to dragging Pierce out by the collar of his shirt.

Lista has clearly tried to remove herself from him multiple times tonight, and he won't take the hint.

He's brushed himself against her, sat directly behind her on the chair, closing his legs around her. And each time, she's moved away. Don't some guys get the fucking hint?

I'd like to personally make sure he gets it next time he tries something funny.

No one else seems to react to her discomfort. If anything, it seems like it's all one big joke that everyone is accepting, but I can see Lista isn't happy and it's twisting my fucking insides. Maybe I'm just looking too deep into it as an outsider.

All I know for certain is that I want to leap across the table and wipe the smug look off Pierce's face.

This time, after Pierce has pissed her off one too many times, Lista leaves the room and goes to the bathroom, announcing her bathroom break rather harshly and exasperated. I take my phone out and text her.

Quin: *Sit with me if you need to.*

Love, In Balance

Nothing more. Nothing less. I don't want her to think I'm getting involved. But I'm here for her. And the thought of her suffering in silence whilst surrounded by people makes me agitated. It'd be the same if I thought anyone was being made to feel uncomfortable by another person. Man or woman. Adult or child. Little or big. Everyone deserves someone in their corner.

A few minutes later she walks back into the living room. I expect she hasn't seen my message. That is until she walks in front of where I'm sat on the couch and sits on the floor, just in front of the gap between my legs.

She knows. She read the text.

I'm fucking stoked that she feels safe with me. I see Pierce gaze over at us. He huffs, shakes his head and knocks his beer back. Jealous prick.

The night continues. We play cards against humanity and then move onto rounds of Mario Kart on the Nintendo switch. Flic and Lista come first and second.

They absolutely whipped our arses and it's so nice to see Lista's face change during her wins.

Oli was right, I needed this, especially when I get to gaze at the most insanely gorgeous girl between my legs.

She doesn't move for most of the night, other than to hide her cards from me during the game.

She playfully nudges my legs when I insult her choice of cards or when I get competitive on Mario Kart. I even fill up her drink for her each time I head into the kitchen. It feels good, and knowing she's safe, away from Pierce helps.

I have to remind my body to chill the fuck out on numerous occasions, because having her so close to me makes me feel things I shouldn't.

My dick twitches at the thought of her touching my thighs or leaning her head back into my lap and looking up at me. I have to refocus my mind onto less appealing things in order to calm the bulge within my jeans. Looking over at Pierce being an arsehole does the job.

   Pierce clearly riles up Lista a few times throughout the night. Her phone goes off whilst she sits near me, and although not meaning to, I see the name Pierce.

I don't look past the name, because it's none of my business, but I can see her tense up each time.

The way he looks at her is scary.

It's a possessive glare that seems unhealthy. It makes me wonder if Pierce and Lista ever had something between them. Inside I'm hoping that's not true.

I'd like to think she has higher standards than some dickhead like him.

   It's 12am when most of us decide to head home.

Oli is staying on Drew's sofa, and Flic sticks around too. Pierce decides that the night is still young, and his beers are still flowing, so he stays for longer. Perhaps he's drowning his sorrows for not getting his own way.

What a shame.

   Pip, Si, Reed, Lista and I all head outside to wait for our rides home. Pip and Reed share one, since they're house mates, which I can imagine is a bunch of fun (*They're both wild*), and Si leaves on his own. He seems like a lone wolf to be honest, so it doesn't surprise me that he departs solo in a cab.

Love, In Balance

Lista and I get another since we live close to each other; Something I discovered during our catchup at Cosy Corner Coffee the other day. Our taxi takes a while to arrive, so we see the guys off safely and wait near the fence under the streetlight until ours arrives. Although we could've waited inside, I think we both wanted to be in the fresh air and away from Pierce.

Lista uses our time to rant about Si, which makes me laugh. He's apparently infuriating, and from what I've witnessed, I can see how he riles up Lista, but it's almost a sibling type relationship with how they bicker. It's weirdly endearing. And seeing them together doesn't make me jealous. Not that I have any right to be, but it's hard to separate that protective side when I'm around Lista. She's captured my mind from day one. That's why I'm so relieved that their relationship is clearly platonic.

I can see her admiration despite the ranting. She talks highly of him and the work he does in chemistry too.

She then moves on to discuss the others and explains how they all know one another from university, despite the age gap. She goes into brief detail about Drew, Pip, Si, Flic and Oli and how they created Five mountains in school before Lista and Pip were '*recruited*' when they all met at the university that has strangely now, brought us together too. It's nice to be let into her world. The guys are awesome, and I can see why they click so well.

When she's finished passionately discussing how annoying, yet awesome she finds them all, that's when I remember I'd forgotten to email Lista earlier about my advisory role for her research. It really doesn't seem appropriate now I've spent an evening with her sat almost

between my legs. She must notice me lost in thought.
"What's up Quin?" she asks gently.

"Lista, I know this is shitty timing. I completely forgot to email you about it when I got home, but Professor Peter's came into the office today. He asked me to be your advisor for your research. He wants me to work with you and guide you through it. If you'd rather not, I can email him first thing when I'm home". She doesn't react at all. She just takes it in and replies thoughtfully.

"I'm more than happy to have you as my advisor. If you're comfortable with it too. If you just let me know what is and isn't ok for you. I know going to a game night and there happening to be a student there isn't great... plus our previous meeting too. I get it if you can't be around me outside of work" she says looking down at her feet.
Although I shouldn't, I can't help myself. I move closer towards her, feeling the heat of our bodies warm the space that falls between us, a stark contrast to the crisp bite of the winter air. I tuck a loose strand of hair behind her ear and move my finger down her jaw, lifting her chin and making her gaze move up to me.
We're face to face, and I wish I could do so much more than just talk to her right now. Her lips, soft as she licks them and then squeezes them together to shield them from the cold. I want to press mine to hers and keep her warm.

"Lista, It's absolutely fine. Like I've said, we knew one another personally prior to professionally. *We* aren't doing anything wrong and I'm more than happy to work with you". I say reassuringly, meanwhile thinking of how the hell I'm going to get through this when all I want to do is crush my body against hers and hear her panting my name. Personally. *Definitely* not professionally.

Chapter 7

Lista
Playlist: *The Middle* – Jimmy Eat World

From: Russell.Q_BiomechEngineering@hotmail.com
Subject: Advisory on biomechanical research project

Callista,

I hope you're well. I hope your weekend has been good so far. I'm just confirming that if you're happy, I will become your advisor during your research project to guide and help you. If we could set up a meeting to go through the work and then plan further calendar dates, that would be great.

I look forward to hearing from you.

Kind regards,

Quin Russell
PhD Biomechanical Engineering Lecturer

Love, In Balance

It's a nice email to wake up to.
Maybe too nice.

I keep thinking about the warmth from his legs Friday night as I sat so closely near the gap between them.
He made me feel secure and safe with his large stature. It's impossible not to.

When I saw his tattoos (*Very unexpected),* My pants may as well have disintegrated right there and then. On the spot. I didn't think I could find him any more appealing than I already did. But when that man walked into Drews kitchen yesterday evening with rolled up sleeves… *damn.*
The anatomically correct heart and brain vertically placed on his forearm, either end of the word *balance* are beautiful.

And when he gripped my outer arm with said inked skin, I'm sure my knees buckled slightly. The smoked whiskey scent I could smell each time he laughed or spoke whilst I was sat in front of him was delicious. Inspiring.
I could've moved back, closer between his legs and lay my head against him. It's been too long since I've been touched, and all I can think about is his hands on me.

I should not be thinking these things right now. He's become my advisor. Plus, he's just being nice to me because he feels sorry for me, clearly. He ghosted me. *Accidently.* And now he's being kind to make me feel less shit about the small, curvy, mediocre looking human being that I am. Makes sense. It's the usual situation. The regular vibe I get from guys. So, I need to distance myself, mentally and emotionally and ensure I stay professional around him. I've totally got this!

I totally don't got this.

We plan to meet up that day to go over the research project and plan the next topics for the sessions.
I find it hard to look at him and be in such close contact as we sit at his desk, facing one another in the office space he hired.

He has his sleeves rolled up again. Ink brands his skin beautifully. I can see the inked brain just below the small portion of skin he's exposing and imagine the rest from what I saw yesterday. Balance between the heart and brain. It speaks to me so deeply. I want to reach out and trace the outline of it to see if I feel anything, but–. Shit I'm lost in thought again.

"Earth to Lista". Quin says, laughing as I snap out of my inner dialogue and realise, he can probably see me staring at his arm.

He raises his eyebrow and licks his bottom lip, before continuing when he sees that I'm now fully paying attention.

"So, are Saturdays and Sundays ok for you to commit to? If not, I understand, but with work and Uni, I don't think a weekday will be viable". I nod.
I decide to stand up, to try and shake the cramps in my residual leg, plus any unwanted thoughts away.

Love, In Balance

I walk around to stand at the side of his desk.

"Yes, honestly that's fine by me. If we could liaise every week about the times, just in case I pick up shifts, that would be great. And if we meet at the coffee shop, if you'd be up for it. It's quiet, cosy and has great food and drink. Plus it won't cost as much as hiring this place" I say, gesturing to the room we're in.

"Yeah absolutely, sounds good. Here's my number, but *please* don't give it to anyone else" He sounds stressed at the thought, almost pleading. "It's my personal number and I really don't want random messages from…" He stops before he can say something and decides against it "random people" he finishes his sentence with.

"Don't worry, I don't speak to people anyway. You can trust me" I tell him, for some unknown reason, putting my hand on his. He looks up at my face and smiles, clasping my hand, rubbing over it gently with his thumb.
"I know I can" he says.

We stay like this for a short while, our hands clasped, gently stroking each-others skin. I get an ache between my legs, wishing he was stroking me elsewhere too.
I'm hoping he feels the same, but then again, surely this isn't good for either of us. His gaze alternates between my eyes and my lips, and I feel myself lose control, so pull back on whatever *this* is between us.
"I best get going anyway. And I'll see you soon" I say as I let go of his hand. He stands with me and walks me to the door, his hand low on my back. We stand so close as we

get to the door. I want to pull him down to me and lock us in this room. Surely this is how porn starts. I've probably come across a few in my time. I'd make him carry me across the room and spread me across his desk.
Shit, I need to leave. I place my hands on his arms and offer a small squeeze. "See you soon Quin".
He looks down at me with the most teasing gaze. "See you soon Lista". It triggers such conflicting thoughts about our relationship. Professional boundaries have already been crossed for our working relationship, but does it count if those crossings happened before working together? My mind is saying *no*. So I think I'll stick with that.

Later that day, I open up my phone to find a message from Pierce. *Ugh.*
Just ugh. I'm sure we've all had the same reaction to that one message that comes through from someone we just really would rather not hear from.

Pierce: *Hey, shame that I'm not your advisor, isn't it? Not sure why they chose Quin. You rarely know him x*

Lista: *I'm fine with him being my advisor. They probably chose him because we don't know each other that well personally.*

Other than kissing each other in a hugely romantic setting and sitting in between his legs at game night. I *don't* say that.
Pierce: *I think we would've worked well together. I know your research ideas. Plus we could've spent more time together. Doesn't mean you can't come to me if you need anything though x*

Love, In Balance

Lista: *I'm fine Pierce. I have Quin to go to with advice on my work now.*

Pierce: *Well, if you need any extra support, you know where to find me sweet cheeks. And let's sort out a day I can take you to dinner x*

I decide against replying to him. Because no.
I wish he'd leave me the fuck alone.
He is consistently following me to my car, in the corridor, around campus and then pinging me with messages every other day.

I wish him and Drew never became acquainted because since then, he's got this fascination with me that is not reciprocated. He scared the shit out of me the other day when I left campus. He snook up on me and wouldn't take no for an answer when he asked me out to dinner.
He knows I'm not interested, but he persists.
He knows how I struggle with intimacy and close contact, and yet still continues to crowd me and touch me.
I'm so sick of his lack of respect for my feelings. I just can't bring myself to mention how I feel to Drew yet.
He won't understand.
He has seen the way Pierce is with me but seems to think it's a joke. I wish he'd see through me and realise how I truly feel. I'm not laughing along with it. I never have.

I can't bear to tell anyone about the other things he's done either. I'm sick of being seen as weak, or as a victim my whole life because of my past. Plus, it's not saying that people will even take me seriously anyway about Pierce. Let's face it. We live in a world where women, amongst

others would rather keep these things under wraps than face the judgement and speculation of people.
Serious allegations are often swept under the rug, so what makes me think that what I have to say about Pierce will be listened to and taken on board.
I know it's unhealthy, but the vault inside my mind is secure, and it's the safest place to keep all of these unwanted memories.
For now.

Chapter 8

Lista

Playlist: *Panic attacks in paradise* - Ashnikko

It's been two weeks since Quin became my advisor.

We've had two sessions off campus, in Cosy Corner Coffee, and they've been successful and productive, despite the immense tension I feel when I'm around him.

He's been as kind as ever, which I can't say for when he's on campus. It's mind boggling to be honest. But I get it.

I had a group of female students come up to me during my lunch break recently to ask me if Quin was a dick to PhD students like me. When I told them *no*, they seemed offended.

One of them even claimed to have slipped him her number whilst discussing her study options. Apparently, he saw it, rolled his eyes and handed it right back to her.

I was internally hysterically laughing. I can just image him doing that. The idea of a student thinking this is acceptable escapes me. They are objectifying him based on his looks and by the sound of it, previous demeanour and causing him discomfort. Not to mention, what happened in the past. The thought of someone as great as Quin having to go through that again makes me sick. Although our history has proven to be potentially crossing professional lines, I'd never approach Quin and make him feel uncomfortable. And what we do *outside* of work is quite frankly no one else's business.

We're two consenting adults. But despite all of this, I'm here to learn and develop my knowledge, and before all else, Quin is vital to my studies right now, and I appreciate the atmosphere between us on campus. When I've been in his lectures, we have no small talk prior or afterwards. Strictly business, which is exactly what it needs to be to prevent me from turning into soup when I see him, to be completely honest. Although I've wanted nothing more than for him to grab my hand again when I go to leave the room and pull me back into his chest, wrapping his arms around me and touching me all over.

Sadly those scenarios have only existed in my mind. I try to keep them in my bedtime thoughts, but they creep in subconsciously whilst I stare at him during lectures.

Sometimes I don't even realise that I've blanked out until something pulls me back to reality. By that point I've missed part of the lecture.

I need to get laid; is what Lilah from Cosy Corner Coffee keeps telling me. Maybe she's right. And you might be thinking, *you talk to your local coffee shop owner about these problems?* Hell yes. Over the years visiting her coffee shop on a weekly basis, she's become my friend. A great one too. We catch up; she tells me her stuff; I tell her mine. It's great, seriously. Highly recommend. Flic joins us too sometimes and we all have a great chat about woman stuff, new coffee flavours for the shop and just general life. This place is the guys usual café too, so Lilah knows we're all here to stay. Each of us consistently recommend Cosy Corner Coffee to friends and family, and over the years business has been good for her. She deserves it.

I digress. *Hugely.*

Speaking of huge. Back to Quin. I suppose he has an effect on most women, and men perhaps. Makes sense after what those girls told me, plus I've heard the comments Oli makes too.

Quin is tall, handsome (although attractiveness is a matter of opinion), and *so* intelligent. He's got everything going for him, and I'm an idiot to think he'd even look at me after our little one-off kiss on New Year's Eve.

He's sweet to me during our time alone, but on campus, he's dominant. Ok, I just felt warmth fill my body at that word. I shiver. But that is exactly what he is. He's dominant, passionate and is here, as a lecturer for a reason. He carries himself with purpose.

He's texted me each Friday to check on my availability for the weekend sessions and he's been so flexible and patient with me. Whilst he's still dominant, he's like a different person off campus, with me.

He's kind, considerate and goes at my pace. If we have meetings or run into each other on campus, he's a lot less lenient. I'm assuming he doesn't want other students to notice him changing when he speaks to me. Not that he does, but he just doesn't act like his grumpy on campus self when we're doing off campus sessions.

Speaking of off campus, It's the STEM university social this evening and I'm not looking forward to being in the same room as so many people.

I'm thankful for Drew and the lads attending.
Despite not working at the university, Reed and Pip are coming too, since they're alumni. The more people I know around me, the better. Flic is busy with work, but she's fired a few texts my way full of random animal gifs to brighten my mind and get those happy chemicals flowing.

Quin will be there too. I can only hope my brain behaves. I don't even want to acknowledge that Pierce will be going, so I'll be avoiding him like the plague.
Then again, I'd probably avoid him more than the latter.
The STEM faculty has a social gathering each year. They have stalls, representation from each topic, and welcome graduate, existing and prospective students.

Last year I was a rep for Engineering and welcomed possible students. It was fun and reminded me of when Reed and I became part of *Five Mountains*. We met Drew and the others at the open day and the rest is history. Keeping the positive history in mind helps me enjoy welcoming new students, despite my lack of joy for socialising.

I do it and push past the anxiety, not only because it's fun and nostalgic, but also because I want to prove to people that no matter what you look like, what gender you are, or what differences you have, you are capable of doing anything you put your mind to.

Little Lista would've loved to have seen a female amputee in STEM when she came to pick her University, so I'm officially now being the person that younger me needed.

Flic always reminds me of the cliché behind the group name and it's helped me overcome many a struggle. She put her thoughts into a poem during her teen years and actually won a poetry contest. It's her claim to fame and I understand why. She quotes it whenever one of us is going through a tough time, and even printed out mini copies on key rings for us all. I keep mine close to me wherever I go. It's my own personal source of motivation throughout life and I'm forever grateful that such a random group name inspired such pure and utter beauty in the form of words.

Five Mountains

You see those mountains that seem to reach the sky,
They never thought they could rise so high.
Starting from nothing and rising through disaster,
After thinking they would crumble and sink thereafter.
Continuing to grow when faced with uncertainty,
Never to know how others see them so perfectly.

So when you're scared of what's ahead,
And you fear the uphill climb,
Remember you are the mountain,
And incredible things take time.

I'm glad to welcome Quin to this year's social since it's his first time. Although we haven't spoken much personally, for good reason, we have texted about tonight and are hoping to catch up in a less work orientated environment. He told me he was looking forward to seeing me... I'm just not sure how to interpret the signals he gives me.

After we held each other's hand and shared a longing stare during our first meeting, I've been distancing myself to try and avoid anymore of whatever this is between us.
It's for the best.

I know that Quin is concerned about people's opinions of him. After what he told me about his journey in lecturing, I understand exactly why he acts the way he does.

He's a young, handsome member of staff, and it's clear that he gets unwanted inappropriate attention from students. You can see it's something that makes him genuinely uncomfortable, and he's quick to make sure he's openly shunting any advances off.

Although, our relationship is a little different I suppose, since we kissed without knowing each-other. And now anything more is clearly off limits. *Sad face.* Although I really do understand why.

I get so nervous about doing or saying the wrong thing to him during our time off campus, and I'm anxious to make the wrong move in general.

I feel like he flirts back with me, but if I cross the line, I'll scare him off. So, I'm hanging back and distancing myself from him. If that's *at all* possible.

I'm at home getting ready. Something which I struggle with hugely.
When I'm on campus for studying or working, my attire makes sense.
When I'm at work on the weekends, I wear my work clothes. But when I go out for events or with friends, I hate choosing an outfit.
I struggle with understanding what is too casual or too

risqué. You know?
I want to look good, but I don't want to be overdressed.

It's difficult being one of the only women in a friendship group, because when I need advice, I'm mostly met with random dude replies that do *not* help me.
Flic rarely messages on the group chat, so I'm often stuck. There are many times she's helped me, but often all I get in situations like this from her on the group chat is a gif. Usually I'm obsessed with them, but times like these I need advice, not hilarious gifs or funny animal videos.

#FiveMountains Group Chat

Lista: Guys, what does one wear to the STEM social this evening? Send help!

Drew: Clothes.

Reed: I second what Drew said.

Oli: I shall be wearing a beige shirt, rolled up sleeves and my brown trousers. I might pop on a fancy jacket too.

*Lista: Oli, thank you for being the only helpful one, but regardless of your reply, it's not helpful for **me**.*
I am a woman. As much as I'd like to wear a shirt and trousers, I actually want to look nice. I do however adore your style, so thank you for sharing x

Pip: *You always look nice. Just wear what you usually wear.*

Lista: *Thanks Pip but dressing for a social is surely different. I don't think people want to see a me wearing my dungarees whilst socialising. Every other person is going to look attractive and beautiful. I want to make a good impression. I don't want to look like the resident engineering troll.*

Drew: *You **are** the resident engineering troll.*

(I hate to say it, but he's not wrong).

Si: *No comment.*

Lista: *You guys are fucking useless. Thanks ever so much. If you ever need help about what to wear, consider me out.*

Si: *I can dress myself perfectly fine. Thanks for the offer though.*

(Si is the single most infuriating human being I've ever met. Although he is one of the most protective too. I love him, but gosh he's an annoying shit)

Lista: *I hate you.*

Si: *I Love you too.*

Love, In Balance

I do genuinely love him.

Lista*: I need some new friends.*

I type all of this with a smile on my face. I love our group dynamic so much. I'm a lucky woman to have such good friends.

Flic: (See— Gif of a monkey slowly peeling a banana)

I end up wearing my black shirt dress with bare legs and my slightly heeled boots.
I have Støtte, my cane, so I feel a little more confident being stood for longer. Plus it helps people to give me some space too.
I'd usually try to cope without for something like this, but my needs are more important than all else.
I have my knee-high socks packed away for when I get tired of prying eyes, and once I've finished welcoming potential newcomers.
It's not that I'm embarrassed of myself and my needs. I love my prosthetic. But in situations with new people, I'd just rather not have to tell the story of my life, injury and all that, twenty times over.
Although I do love making up incredible stories to my nieces and nephews every time they ask me questions about it. I am naughty.
I pair the outfit with my black blazer and a black belt with gold details.
I lightly curl my hair and even put on a gold necklace and my dangly dopamine and serotonin earrings hanging from

my stretchers. I feel nice.
Despite not knowing what to wear, and having zero helpful input from the guys, I feel good.
I'm not too casual and not too dressed up, so win-win! Plus, I still feel professional.

The event seems to have some very non-professionally dressed groups of people. When I first turned up, the outside made me feel like I was on a night out, rather than an organised event run by a university.

Many students in younger years are showing more than necessary for a social open evening.
Quin may be in for some attention this evening.

These people look good, don't get me wrong, but the vibes I'm getting from them are that of club goers.

Maybe I'm just jealous of the tremendous cleavage, perfectly sculpted backsides and flawless makeup.
Perhaps.

Drew and the guys are all dressed smart-casual.
Shirts, smart shoes and some of them in blazers too. They look good. I'm proud to be with them. Well, other than pierce, who is currently chatting up said club goers and pretending to be more important than he actually is.
Thankfully he hasn't yet noticed me.
He turned up *after* my talk, so unbeknownst to him, I'm not here. So I'm trying to blend in as I make my way to the bar, and hopefully for the rest of the evening.
If it wasn't for my rather 'out there' lower leg, I'd be great at blending in. But, as I've learnt throughout my life. It's good to stand out and be your own person.
Pip reminds me of this consistently. He is the most unapologetically authentic person I have ever met.

Unapologetically himself. I wouldn't change a thing about him, or any of the guys for that matter.
I'm happy to deal with the occasional infuriating things that they do.

I get to the bar without being seen by a certain dickhead and grab myself a drink whilst chatting briefly with Professor Peters about Quin being my new advisor.

He wishes me well and says what a good team Quin and I make.

"You two are both so alike. He will be able to shed tremendous light on biomechanical topics. He's one of the brightest young lecturers and biomechanical engineers I know Lista. I can see great things coming from your partnership for this research".

He seems to think highly of Quin. It's nice to hear. I certainly think highly of him too. *Wink wink.*

"I agree. It's going very well so far. Quin's been a huge help. I'm grateful for you putting me on his schedule. I couldn't have asked for a better advisor".

"Did you and Quin know each other prior to meeting on campus? You seem to naturally have a good rapport considering the little time you've known one another" He asks.

For some reason his question makes me nervous. I don't want to say something wrong or get Quin into trouble.

"We met briefly on New Year's Eve. We both happened to be out of the city on a break and our paths crossed. It was a pleasant surprise to see that he's a lecturer here" I say. Hoping I've not made the wrong move. Honesty is the best policy after all, right?

"I had a feeling you both knew one another. I've never seen two people get on so well instantly. I look forward to seeing more from you both".
He looks over my shoulder and smiles. Raising his eyebrows.
"I'll leave you to it anyway Lista" he says, placing a warming hand on my shoulder as he walks past me.
Quin appears from behind me, lightly brushing my back with his hand as he walks to stand next to me.

"Evening" he says to me pleasantly.

"Hey. You just missed Professor Peters".

"I just saw him as he walked away. He gave me a nice pat on the shoulder. You look *great* by the way" he says to me. His eyebrows lifting as his eyes scan my body.

I feel heat rise to my cheeks.
"Oh, thank you. I was panicking whilst choosing an outfit. And the guys were useless. Oli tried, but his idea of helping me choose an outfit was just him telling me what he's wearing" I say laughing. He laughs with me. "And I'm not sure I'd quite rock a man's baggy shirt the way you guys do". I notice him swallow intensely.

I'm definitely not thinking of wearing Quins shirt, with nothing else on… I snap out of it almost instantly.

"I mean, the other women here look beautiful. I'm just not like them" I say laughing "It took me ages to figure out an outfit that was a balance of casual, smart, professional and appealing. I mean, I've turned up like this but seen countless younger students looking… I'm not really sure how to describe it" I say with a laugh under my breath.
I realise how much I've been speaking and how little I've come up for air. It's time to let him get a word in.

Quin looks over my outfit, lingering a while longer than necessary, his hand still grazing my lower back. He leans in close to my ear.

"Well, I think you look great Lista. I'm not sure many others got the brief to be honest". I can feel his stubble brush against my face before he pulls back. I shiver.

"Well Quin, you look great too. I'm partial to rolled up shirt sleeves and tattoos" I say, perhaps coming across a little too flirtatious.

"Well thank you. I'm glad to see your legs on full show. It's breathtaking Lista." he says whilst looking at me with hooded eyes. For a moment I wonder what he means, but then realise he's talking about my prosthetic. That is until he continues.

"They both are" he says, smiling into his drink. He's flirting back.
Now I feel a little flushed. And lost for words. That's a rarity.

"Cheers to that" I say.

We stand around talking for a while, killing the time before attending the lecturers talks.
Quin stays with me, completely by choice it seems.
I give him multiple chances to go off and do as he pleases, but he chooses to be my companion throughout.
I'm definitely not complaining.

So far, I've done my own small talk and sat through Oli and Drew's. They did a joint discussion about a collaboration they did recently, showing how STEM departments work alongside one another.
I've also just sat in on Si's too.
I love Chemistry, but watching Si deliver on the topic is annoying. I love him, but he is a know it all, and I'm forever hearing about his research on the group chat and whenever we get together. It's like I already know everything he's discussed at his talk, because he's run it by me before multiple times. It *is* astonishing though.
After a difficult time in his life, he turned to Chemistry and now he's turned it into his career. He's in the midst of a successful business start-up in drug development and I couldn't be prouder.
I was forced into also enduring Pierce's talk too. There's only so long you can fake going to the toilet for. Drew definitely would've called me out on it.
Thankfully it's over and I'm just standing around before meeting the guys. I feel a little strange and anxious when a group of younger students approach me. But I put on my

welcome face and am excited to discuss the different engineering pathways with them.

"Hey, are you part of engineering" a young woman asks me.

"Hello. Yes, I'm a PhD student in mechanical engineering. Is there anything I can help you with?" I say in response. Burnt out, but excited to potentially offer insight.

"Oh, no, we're fine. We just thought you were a lecturer or professor. We noticed you with the other lecturers and Professors earlier and were intrigued. So, you're a student who hangs out with teachers? I bet that's fun" she says with a huge girly grin. Laughing with the other girls. Ok this conversation is just bizarre. It's becoming quite obvious now, who's here for the right and wrong reasons.

"Oh, I suppose yes. My group of friends happens to comprise of a few STEM academic staff. I've known them since beginning my studies at the university. They were fellow students of mine, prior to becoming staff, so I suppose I've never seen it like that". Is all I can think to say. Not that I owe them an explanation at all.

"Maybe we should get all cosy with the lecturers" the woman who appears to lead her little group says, "It's always been a fantasy of mine" They all laugh.
I do not laugh.

"Especially Dr Quin Russell. I wouldn't mind being cosy with him" the other woman says.

As if on cue, Quin appears from behind me and lightly squeezes my arm.

"Sorry if I'm interrupting. Lista, your drink" he says as he hands me my well needed beverage. Now that discussions are over, it's safe to have a cheeky tipple.

"Thanks Quin. I was just explaining my relationship with the lecturers to this group of students. They thought I was a fellow member of staff like you, Drew, Si, and Oli".

"And Dr Pierce" the woman interrupts.

I get agitated and tense up. I feel like Quin tenses slightly too for some reason.

"Oh, and Quin, this student was *particularly* interested in your role and our relationship too" I say with a pissed off expression.

Quin rolls his eyes. This is the kind of inappropriate bullshit that Quin is sick of.

"I bet you get an advantage, being so friendly with them all" she says. And that's when I freeze and feel the anger boil within me. Would a man be treated like this if he were in my situation?

I flip.

"If you're insinuating that my academic success has anything to do with my personal relationships with members of the university staff, I'd appreciate you rethinking. I've worked my way up as a disabled woman in STEM and done a good job of it without the need to rely on *any* men. Hell, I have less limbs than any of them and I've still managed to become a success. As I have already said, I've been friends with the lecturers, even Dr Quin prior to them becoming lecturers here. So, I'd appreciate you just stop this nonsense now. Because I'm not having my reputation questioned by people who don't know me. If you need to become *friendly*" I say sarcastically "with the lecturers in order to achieve academic success, be my guest. But exclude me from this narrative. And a little food for thought for your clearly narrow minds, would you have questioned a male on this?" they look at each other in shock, the thought clearly circling in their stubborn little heads.

"Yeah, I thought so". I say as I walk away.
I look at Quin with a sorry expression as I walk past him.

It's not the first time I've been questioned and undermined by someone due to being a woman or being disabled, or just choosing a career in STEM, but it still stings.
I work hard. I don't deserve arseholes treating me like shit, as though they have a right and reason to.

I've learnt to walk away from these things for my own sake. I can reflect when I'm in a more neutral mindset.

I head towards a vacant bar table, place my drink on it and stand there, catching my breath and regaining composure.
Just when I think I can breathe again, I'm thrown straight back on edge again by two hands squeezing my waist, followed by a whisper in my ear.

"Look at you being a cock tease. You look insane Lista". The smell of alcohol is strong on his breath. He makes me feel disgusting. I want to teleport home, out of this moment

and curl up away from the world.
It's too much for one day. I can't take much more.
 Is what I'm wearing too sexy? This is my fault, isn't it?...
For just being a woman. I'm a shame to my sex.
I start to panic internally, feeling my blood pressure rise. I begin to spiral, feeling trapped.
 "Pierce, please don't" I manage to say through my feelings of disgust at myself.
He's pressing up against my ass and my back. I can feel him press his lower region against me harder.

 "How can I not when you look like *this*. You're the one who turned up looking this fucking good" he says as he kisses my neck, nipping my skin slightly, and then squeezes my arse before walking away after whispering into my ear "I'll make sure to find you later and feel you again".
It is my fault.
My thoughts are spiralling dangerously, and I feel like I'm losing control. My head starts to feel strange.
I feel foggy and disconnected from reality, almost.
I stand still for a moment, trying my hardest to breathe.
I'm a statue of disgust, reminding every woman around me what *not* to be. I'm an embarrassment to women in STEM.
My panic worsens. I can feel my insides start to shake.
The familiar hands around my throat, restricting my breathing.
My breath becomes rapid and everything around me becomes louder. I can feel my skin brushing against the fabric of my clothes. The smell of alcohol, a mixture of everyone's perfume and heavy air floods my senses.

Love, In Balance

I need to leave.
I *need* to leave.

I'm not fully aware of myself, as if I'm in a fever dream. Things are hazy, like I'm on a battlefield full of fog and overwhelming noise.
I half stumble, half walk out the doors briskly and make my way to the side of the building out of sight. I'm unsure of how long I stand there.
Seconds. Minutes maybe.
But out of nowhere a hand lands at my forearm, brushing it lightly. I react in the only way I can right now, screaming out. I am in pure survival mode and all of my reactions I can rarely claim as my own, since they happen without prior consent from my usual self.
I can't speak or make sense of anything around me.
I'm crying now. I don't see who is with me because my mind is spinning, but I can imagine it's Pierce.
He's cornered me. I'm unsafe, alone and away from people. He can do what he wants with me like before.
I need to escape. As I try to flee, rapidly breathing, wobbly on my feet, moaning in pain from the sensory overload, I feel warm arms around me pulling me just tight enough to feel grounded but not crowded.

It's not Pierce. He doesn't touch me like this. I'm safe.

"It's me. Callista, you're ok. It's Quin. You're safe sweetheart. I'm here".

I melt into the big wall that happens to be Quins body. He continues holding me, only releasing me with one arm briefly.

The next thing I know, I'm surrounded by Drew, Oli, Reed, Pip and Si. I'm sat at a table outside, well away from the building where everyone resides. Drew is sat next to me on my left-hand side, drawing gentle circles on my back whilst I come back to reality as the seconds go by.

Si is sat on my right, acting like he doesn't care, but under the table has his hand on my leg to show he's there whilst letting me lean on his shoulder. The others are sat around the table, concerned.

I notice Quin walking away in the distance.

"I'm sorry. I just tried to leave. I needed to go home. I didn't want to burden anyone" I say through tears and panicked breaths.
Drew places his hand over mine.

"Lista, in the nicest way possible, shut the fuck up. Quin noticed you leave in a hurry and came to see if you were ok. You had a panic attack and I'm assuming sensory overload. He wanted to make sure you felt safe.
He texted me as soon as he could to let me know what was going on. He made sure you were safe with us before heading off".

I'm so confused. Why isn't he staying. Have I annoyed him?
"Why isn't he here Drew?".
"Lista, he was worried that you didn't feel safe around him. He noticed how you reacted when he first approached you. He wanted you to be surrounded by us, so that you'd feel at ease".
Shit. I've fucked up.

The guys see me into a taxi before heading back into the event. Pierce is standing waiting for them, looking over at me. I dip my head and sink into the taxi seat, hoping he didn't notice me.

"I need to change the destination if that's ok" I say to the driver.

"Of course. Where would you like to go?" says the nicest taxi driver I've ever met. Seriously I felt myself relax just by getting into the car. How is that even a thing. Vibes and all.

The taxi ride was nice, and certainly needed. I used the journey to come back to my neutral mindset. This included discussing how incredible the vegan treats are at Cosy Corner Coffee with the taxi driver the entire journey.
It was a *must* after discovering a mutual love for the café.
I mean, what better to brighten your spirits and ground you than the thought of a good coffee and slice of cake?

When we arrive at my destination, I get out of the taxi, walk up to the house with haste and ring the doorbell. Quin opens the door, and his face is a picture; Shock, concern and anger, but mostly filled with worry. He looks... distressed.

"Lista, what are you doing here? … Get inside" he says forcibly, but full of compassion and care.
He guides me in, his hand on my lower back.
His house is beautiful.

Cream walls, surrounding a dark deal accent wall. Black and grey comfortable furniture.
Clean, decluttered and slick, but still warming and homely.
He guides me to the sofa and places a blanket at my side.

"Give me a minute Lista", he says before walking into a room that I assume is the kitchen.
I can't help but feel calm here. I feel…safe, warm and at ease. I sigh in relief as that feeling of ease encompasses my body. I feel content being with Quin, knowing I can explain to him how I *do*, in fact, feel safe with him.
Since I made him feel shitty earlier.

I look around and notice the table in the centre of the room is topped with a neat pile of books and a plant.

The TV is playing relaxing music, with a beautiful winter scene displayed on the screen, and there is a book on the arm of the sofa with a bookmark in it too. He must have been reading before I kindly disturbed him.
There's something so attractive about a guy who reads.

He comes back a few minutes later with two mugs topped with cream.
He places them on the table in front of the sofa and sits closely beside me, but still honouring my space enough to let me breathe.

"Lista, you should be at home. Why are you here?... you know what, that doesn't matter. I'm sorry" he says, closing his eyes and sighing deeply. "Look, something clearly happened earlier and all I wanted was for you to be ok. So, I guess I'm just confused that you're here", he says calmly, looking down at his legs.

Love, In Balance

"Quin, I had to make sure you knew that I feel safe around you. Drew told me you left earlier after he and the guys arrived because you wanted me to feel safe. I couldn't bear the thought that you felt shit. I… I". and there it goes again.

Words stuck, tears filling my eyes and the overwhelming feeling that I'm the one to blame for this entire night. My eyes are shut as I ground myself, tapping into my logical mind to avoid a panic attack being triggered. That's when I feel a comfortable heaviness at my core.

Quin has placed a hot water bottle in my lap, against my abdomen. His hand gently placed on top of my left shoulder.

"Focus on your breathing, Lista. I'm here. It's ok". I open my eyes and meet his hand with mine. Both resting gently upon my shoulder.

"I'm just…sorry Quin".

He moves closer to me. Being here, inside the walls of his welcoming home, with him is the perfect amount of stimulation. It's calming, visually decluttered, audibly comforting and a beautiful temperature. I'm not overwhelmed or crowded, and the more time I sit here, with him near, I slowly heal.

"Lista, you have nothing to apologise for. All I want is for you to feel ok. So just breathe, relax and try to empty your mind of worry. I'm ok. In fact, I'm even better now that I can make sure you're ok". He leans toward the table and passes me the mug. It's hot chocolate.

The feeling of familiarity fills me with comfort. Every time I've been with Quin, we've shared a hot chocolate.

There's something odd about it that grounds me and pulls me back to earth. He gets me. And a mutual love for warm beverages is enough to bring anyone together.

We talk for hours before he gets me a taxi home. I avoid bringing up what triggered my episode though. It's my fault anyway, so I'll just process it in my mind, lock it inside that vault and do what I always do; Act like everything is 'A ok'. I'm scared he'll think it was all just me hugely overreacting, so it's easier to just keep my lip sealed.

Despite the holding back on my end, something beautiful does happen though. He asks me a question that means a lot to me.

"Lista. I just need to ask you something. As bizarre as it may seem to ask this. Are you ok with hugs?".

My heart warms. I'm rarely asked by anyone about this. They just assume I'm happy with physical contact, and I'm too proud to say otherwise.

"I'm sorry if this is an awkward thing to ask, but I'm just so worried about making you feel uncomfortable, and if you ever need me in situations like earlier, the last thing I want to do is make you feel worse. I know some people feel worse when they're hugged, so I guess I just want to hear it from you so I know how to be there for you in the best way I can". A tear comes to my eye again.

"Quin, that's really kind of you to ask. Usually, I don't like hugs unless it's from people I trust". He puts his head down, sighing. Until I continue what I was saying.

"And I trust you Quin. When I realised it was your arms

surrounding me earlier when I was panicking, I immediately knew I was safe. When I came around from the episode and saw you walking away, I needed to come back to you, hence why I came here. I needed you to know how safe I felt when you were with me".

The next thing I know, he's moved closer to me and wrapped his arms around me.
I wrap mine around his and we melt into each other before he loosens his grip and leans his forehead against mine.
Our faces are so close and my heart races.
I wish he'd grab my face and kiss me right here, but I think I've honestly had enough excitement for one day.
He pulls back and looks into my eyes. We hold each other's gaze, but his eyes keep trailing down to my lips.
He looks pained and hungry, as though he's struggling to keep himself at bay, but pulls away, looking down.
It's a good job he has it all together, because my mindset right now is not the steadiest and I may do things I regret.

Although I'd love to sink into him even more and lose myself to his big, warm body, I have so many things that need to be considered. Right now is not the time to do so. Not after everything that has happened today.

So I also pull back and lift my mug, finishing off my hot chocolate. The calming music setting the scene.
I leave shortly after, full of confusion from everything about today.

Chapter 9

Lista
Playlist: *The Only Exception* - Paramore

It's Saturday.
I'm thankful to be at work, occupied, so that I have little time to actually think about what happened yesterday at the faculty social.

I left Quins late last night and practically collapsed onto my bed. Being in Quins arms made me feel like I'd found my safe place, but I'm trying not to think about it too much. He is my lecturer after all and he's so quick to make sure personal relationships stay away from campus.

It still doesn't stop me wanting to be around him all the time though. I'm just finishing off the last few bits at my part-time job. I've been helping fix some machinery and perform maintenance tasks.

It's been a rather sweaty day so far and I've been pretty hands on since I'm one of the only engineers on site today. It's kept my mind from spiralling though, so all is good.
I clock off at 1pm thankfully. I know what you're thinking. Lucky you, finishing at 1pm. Give me a break.

Love, In Balance

It's Saturday and I've been at work since 5am. After *everything* that happened yesterday.

I'm mentally and physically exhausted, and I still have to work through a long ass session with Quin this afternoon.

I open my phone to message Quin and see a text update about a parcel being delivered.

Parcel Delivery: *Miss Harper, your order is running late. It will now be delivered between 4pm and 7pm.*

Fuck. Sake.

It's always the case, isn't it?

Lista: *Hey Quin, I'm clocking off at 1pm from work. I'm really sorry but I've just had a message about a parcel being delayed. It's now expected between 4pm and 7pm so I can't leave the house. By the time I get home from work it'll be about 1.45pm and I'd have to get ready. I'll end up being at Cosy Corner about 3pm, which means we'd have an hour to work, so do you want to cancel? I'm so sorry! This is not like me at all.*

It takes about one minute for his response.

Quin: *Let's do the session at yours if you're comfortable with me coming over. I can drive to you in 10 minutes, so any time suits me when you've gotten home and wound down a bit. If not, just say, but I'm more than happy to continue with the session. The location is irrelevant* ☺

Quin Russell. In *my* home. What a dangerous scenario. Especially after last night. I can still feel the bliss my body experienced when I was wrapped in his arms.

I agree to it anyway.

Lista: *As long as you're ok with it, so am I. Would you be ok to come over at around 4/4.15pm. Just so I can make myself less smelly and more presentable. I've been working since 5am and it is horribly obvious by my appearance* ☺

Quin: *Send me your address and I'll see you later* ☺

He arrives at 4.15pm. I've had enough time to shower thankfully, otherwise I would have personally offended his nostrils with the scent of my body. No one wants that.
I now smell like strawberry and vanilla, thanks to my lush perfume.

I'm nervous about having Quin in my home. This is where I sleep, shower, wee, cry, pass wind… and it feels overwhelming. I'm scared that my professionalism may dwindle in the comforts of my home.

Also, it just occurred to me that it's Saturday night. The majority of work sessions are on the weekend. Does Quin also not have anything better to do?
I guess it does make me feel slightly better about my lack of weekend life.

He's wearing a casual cream shirt with the top two buttons undone. His sleeves are rolled up, revealing his ink kissed skin. His casual jeans are tucked into doc martens.
Omg.

Love, In Balance

How is he insanely intelligent, kind, handsome and fucking stylish. *This man.* He comes in and takes his shoes off. *Gentlemanly.*
He's so big compared to my doorframe. Why am I picturing him picking me up and pushing me against it. I really do need to stop. This is the kind of thing I was talking about! A dangerous mindset whilst in my own personal space.

"Welcome to my home. I'm sorry to have changed plans so late. This *stupid* package. Thanks for giving me some time to make myself less… ew". His jaw tightens and he seems to hold his breath for a few seconds.

"It's no problem having our session here. If anything, there'll just be less distractions". He says. *Yeah sure.* Less distractions. Other than the fact that a fucking gorgeous man is in *my* house.

"I'd image it's quieter than the coffee shop, and plus we can be as loud as we want –." he says but immediately realises how it sounds…we both stand with our eyes wide.

Luckily that's when itty bitty kitty Edith comes walking in. She's finished crunching on her cat treats and now she's interested in seeing who our guest is.
Our very handsome, well dressed, smoky scented, lusciously low-voiced guest.
I'm grateful for her waltzing in and saving that… moment. He bends down and she headbutts his hands.

"Well, hello there. It's good to meet you. I'd image you're the boss of the house" he says to Edith whilst glancing up at me with a smile and raised eyebrows whilst running his hand gently over her shiny coat.

"I should've warned you that I have a cat before you came over, in case you were deadly allergic, but I'm assuming you're not, right?".

He laughs.
 "Well, I have a cat, so if I were, I'd be fucked".
I feel my body shiver when he swears in his deep, smooth, delicious voice.

"Awhh, I didn't become acquainted with them yesterday. Maybe next time" I say and again, feel awkward.
Why would I ever need to go to Quins house again.
 "Well, meet Edith. My home bestie".

"Edith it's good to meet you. I wonder if you're named after a certain famous female engineer" he says as he looks up at me.

"You are most certainly right" I say, as my ovaries are clearly having a moment to themselves to celebrate the proximity of such a fucking delightful gentleman who knows about female engineers.

"Oh, and you can definitely meet Edison next time you come over" he says, before standing to his full height and waiting for me to lead the way.

Love, In Balance

I pull a knowing face at him as he emphasized the word Edison. He's also named him cat after an engineer. Where is this man from? And why did I get so lucky to meet him?

We work in my living room on the sofa for a while, using my nest tables to work on.
Eventually we give in and sit on the floor so we're closer to the table. Saving our backs and necks in the long run.
It's actually been very productive so far. I thought it'd be weird, but it's nice.

My doorbell goes off, pulling us out of deep thought. I jog to the door and start bringing in the parcels. Quin appears and starts helping me.

"Don't worry Quin, I can manage" I say through strained breathing as I carry the first parcel.

"I know you can manage, but it'll be quicker if I help".

Once we've brought them all in, I head to refill the drinks. Making good use of the time I can stretch my legs after being cross legged on the floor for an hour.
My leg started to cramp so the relief is wonderful.

"Need any help" Quin says from behind me.

"I was just going to grab us both another drink. Anything in particular you'd like?".

"Hmm" he think's dramatically, rubbing his chin. "What do you stock in this fine establishment?" he ends up saying.

I laugh.

"Well, I have a coffee machine. I make a delicious hot chocolate. I have herbal tea, regular tea, soft drinks, juice, squash, filter water or something stronger. Is that a good enough list sir?".
Well, calling him sir was a weird call. Considering he's technically my tutor.

"What are you having on this fine Saturday evening?" he asks me.

"Well, I wasn't going to drink anything alcoholic due to working, but it should be ok to have one. It is Saturday after all. Care to join me?" I say.

He winks.
"Sounds good".

It's been another hour since we sat down to start working again. We've managed everything from the list we set ourselves, so start to wind down and put things away.
Quin asked me a few questions about my prosthetic and his interests made me feel so much more settled. He even asked if I needed to remove it to give my residual leg a rest.
As much as I'd love to, it makes getting around the house harder and I'd rather not have to use my crutches.
Plus I removed it earlier after work and had a good few hours of relief. The sentiment was lovely, as usually people would prefer that I keep my prosthetic on.
It just makes me like Quin even more.

"What are those parcels by the way? When you said waiting in for a parcel, that was *not* what I had in mind?".

"Oh, it's two separate chests of drawers. I chose to avoid the extortionate amount for someone else to make it for me, so I'm putting it together myself. And yeah, they're fairly large parcels. Hence why I needed to be in for them to be delivered" I say rolling my eyes.

"Building furniture is great. I loved putting it all up when I moved into my house".

"Feel free to help" I say jokingly.

"I'd be happy to. Let's do it. We're finished with our session, so I'm happy to stay and help. I'm just glad your place doesn't have stairs. Saves a lot of hassle having to drag them up". He says, deadly serious.
The perks of living in a ground floor flat.

"*Tonight?* I mean, I'm super impatient with things like this so I *was* planning on doing it when we'd finished work, but I don't want to make my problem, yours. Plus, we haven't eaten. This is going to take a few hours. And Quin, you could do more damage to your ribs and hand".

"Like I said, I love doing this stuff. I have nothing better to do. And we could just order food. Or I'm happy to grab something when I get home" he says with no hesitation at all. Also avoiding my nudge about his broken and bruised ribs.
He actually wants to stay and put up with me for longer.

He's a saint. Or does he just feel bad again?

"I never say no to takeout, but only if you're sure that you're ok staying, and if you're sure you'll be ok. I know you like to keep work and personal life separate, so I don't want you to feel uncomfortable being around me for anything other than work".

"Lista, if this is about what those students said, please don't worry. I'm happy to be around you. *More* than happy. On campus, we're professional. Outside, we're... us. And it's no one's business but our own. My ribs will hold up. I'm not exactly engaging in a full body workout" I blush "Plus, right now I wouldn't want to be anywhere else".

Chapter 10

Quin
Playlist: *'Save tonight'* – Eagle-eye Cherry

I've been at Lista's since 4.15pm.
It's now 7.30pm.
We've gotten through the work session and now I'm sipping an old fashioned that Lista made me whilst helping her build furniture.

We briefly discovered our shared interest of *The Holiday*, so we've now put it on in the background.
She didn't even make fun of me for being a fan of a great romance film.

I genuinely don't think I'd rather be doing anything else.
Her apartment is great; It's comfortable, warm and the kind of place I imagined she'd have.
It's minimal and decluttered, but cosy, with a mixture of natural dark woods, dark furniture, beige walls and pops of burnt orange. The fairy lights and candles add such a calming atmosphere, and Edith is nestled between a set of soft pillows and a fluffy throw on the sofa. It feels like a home. I could quite happily see myself here with her often.

I'm pulled out of my thoughts when she gently places the hammer down on the unfinished chest of drawers whilst she readjusts her position.

"What are you thinking about?" a gentle voice asks me. I regain control of my mind and come back to reality.

"Sorry" I say softly, snapping out of my thoughts. "I'm just content. I was appreciating your apartment. It's homely. Thanks for having me".

"Thank you. That means a lot. I thought I'd be burdening you with having to work here, so I'm pleased to hear that. It's been a pleasure having you" she says as she sips her old fashioned.

We've ordered food and kept the drinks coming. I'm not drunk or even tipsy, but I'm feeling relaxed and slightly merry. My mind is looser than usual and I'm appreciating Lista even more than I do normally.

It's dangerous territory.

I'm still trying to remain professional, but this evening feels out of the professional boundaries and my body has a mind of its own.

Just in the nick of time, as I go to lean forward towards Lista, disaster saves me from doing something I may have regret.

"Fuck. Shit!" accidently leaves my mouth when the hammer Lista just placed on the table slips off and onto my hand, shattering the glass I was drinking from.

The shards of glass fly between us both and my first concern is her.

Lista leans toward me.

"Fuck Quin, I'm so sorry. that was my fault. I'm so sorry" she says panicking.

"Lista, are you hurt? Do you have glass on you" I say as I lightly graze her arms with my right hand.

Love, In Balance

We're both covered in Whiskey and there are small shards of glass in her right arm and on her legs. I've got some in my left hand and on my trousers, alongside a cut in my palm. We both stand. She helps me get up from the floor and we walk towards the bathroom.

"I'm fine Quin, just a few shards. I'm so sorry". She rests her hand gently on the one I've cut.

"There's blood on your shirt Quin. Let's start removing the shards and then get your hand bandaged up. *As if you've got another hand injury after just healing from your last injury*" she says as she stands close to me, removing the shards of glass bit by bit from my hand and wrist, shaking her head and looking worried.

"Lista I'm ok. It's not your fault. The hammer just slipped". She doesn't respond, and just continues nursing my hand.

"Hold put" she says suddenly.
She runs to the kitchen, reaches into the cupboard, grabs the first aid box and runs back into me.

She opens up the box, standing close to me again and cleans the cut on my palm gently, before wrapping a small bandage around my hand tightly. She seems to know exactly what she's doing.

"You seem well practised at this" I say curiously, trying to lighten the mood.
She smiles and raises her eyebrows.

"It's a good job isn't it? After the accident, I wanted to ensure I could learn lifesaving skills. So I've had extensive first aid training and keep up to date with it each year where I can. It sure comes in handy. Now, without sounding weird Quin, you need to take your clothes off". Heat crawls up my body and my eyes widen.

"Is this also part of the first aid training?" I ask, jokingly.

She laughs and shakes her head at me.

"I'll have to take mine off too once I've taken the glass out. We'll need to give everything a good shake outside and bag yours up. We're both covered in shards. It's not safe. Plus, we'll end up getting them all over the floor if we continue walking around in these clothes, and I don't want to put kitty Edith in danger too".

I'm still not sure what to say so I just go with what comes to mind.

"Lista, I don't have anything else to wear, and I'm pretty sure being in just my boxers in your house isn't going to make either of us feel too comfortable". I probably shouldn't have said that.

She blushes deeply, smiling and looking anywhere but at me.

"Let me remove the glass from myself and I'll see what I can find" she says whilst examining her arm. I move across to her and start helping her remove the tiny pieces of glass sticking out of her skin.

It aggravates me to know that her perfect fucking skin is injured.

"I'm not sure if you've noticed but I'm quite a lot bigger than you in clothes size" I say, trying to lighten the mood.

Love, In Balance

She looks up.
I've managed to make her smile. Our eyes meet and we look at each other for a few seconds before she responds. The tension between us is nothing I've felt before. It's distracting.

"*Obviously* I'm not going to give you *my* clothes, you big dummy" she says whilst giving my chest a little tap "I think I have some spare tucked away from when Reed came over to help me decorate. Long story, but I bought everyone clothes to paint in so they wouldn't get their clothes messy. Reed left his here. *Luckily*. Also, you don't need to help me Quin. You can just relax your hand. I won't be long".

She's so adamant about me not helping, but she's not winning this.

"Lista, I'm making sure you're ok. You were *also* covered in glass, and I'd rather stand here and help you, than risk you being injured".
We stand in silence until each shard is removed from her.

We walk into her room, and she slowly starts unbuttoning my shirt.
Not at all how I imagined this evening to go.
And if I did imagine this scenario, it would *not* be because I was covered in glass.

"I'm sorry. This is so weird, but your hand is hurt, and you need this shirt off", she says apologetically.

She's stood so close to me; I can feel the warmth of her breath on the skin of my abdomen.

She gently pulls my shirt open and then peels it off of me, slowly.

She has to lean closer and reach up to get my shirt off, over my shoulders and down my arms, since our height and builds are so different. I can see that she's trying not to look at my body, but her eyes trace the tattoos on my right arm. I can feel heat rushing through my body with her this close.

"Holy shit Quin, I know Edward said you had bruised and broken ribs, but I didn't realise how bruised your abdomen would be" she says as she gently runs her slightly calloused fingers across my bruises. It's heavenly.
"How do you feel now? It looks so sore" she says.

I take her hand that's on my bare abdomen and gently graze my thumb over it.
"I'm ok now Lista". Blood rushes through my veins and I'm so tempted to pull her into me. The tension is sweet, but when we both realise that we've been silent for a while, touching each other, we snap out of it.
She looks down and then back up to me, running her fingers across my arms to feel for glass.
"Do you feel any shards on your skin or are you ok?" she asks me.

"No all good" I say, although wishing there was some way to prolong this moment between us.
She grabs some clothes from inside the bottom drawer and passes them to me.
"If you turn around, we can both get changed. Then we can sort our glass covered clothes if that's ok?".
Turning around and removing my trousers, knowing she's

undressing behind me is immense. I really did not expect this evening to end up like this.

"That's fine Lista. As long as you feel comfortable with me being in the room".
She looks at me reassuringly.
"I trust you Quin".
The trousers she has given me fit ok.
They're men's dark grey jogging bottoms. They're a little on the small side, which I gathered, since Reed is slimmer than I am, but it's better than my clothes being full of glass. I'm a little worried the trousers are a quite... figure hugging in the dick region, but there's not much I can do right now. The T-shirt is plain black and again, it's snug. I don't usually wear tight clothing, so this is a first. It definitely leaves nothing to the imagination.
Like *seriously*, nothing.

"Ouch. shit". I hear her mutter under her breath.

"Are you ok?" I ask, concerned. Still making sure to keep my eyes away from her.

"Yeah, I think some of the glass came off my shirt whilst I took it off. I can feel a sore spot on my upper back and on my collar bone".

"Do you need me to take a look?" I say hesitantly.
"Erm, if you could, please" she says.
I can feel her blushing from here. I turn to see her lifting her top and exposing her back. She has the most incredible tattoo down her spine, from the base of her neck, going past

the waistband of her joggers that hug her waist. I assume it reaches the bottom of her back.

There are whisps of ink peering from around her ribs. I can just see them slightly. I want to kiss them.

Shit, I can't be thinking like this. She trusts me, and I'm her friend before anything else. But fuck, she's insanely beautiful.

Her body is a powerhouse. An hourglass with scars and stretch marks that paint her history on her skin. It's breathtaking.

I touch her upper back delicately with my fingertips, brushing away loose strands of hair.

She winces when I lightly graze over the sore area where a shard of glass has stuck in her skin. I pick it out and place it in the bin to the side.

"I've taken out that piece. Feel any better? Let me check for others".

She nods in reply. I smooth the edge of my finger over the surface of her back. She shivers as I move across a sensitive part, goosebumps raising over her skin, under my fingers. Both of our breathing gets deeper.

"Your back is all good" I say, as I unroll her top, covering her back up.

I move around to face her.

The front of her top is low cut and held up, over her shoulders by thin spaghetti straps, exposing her chest and neck.

"Let me check your collarbone" I say, gently, worried I might scare her off. She stretches up slightly to close the distance between us, as I bend down. She gathers her hair and moves it over to one shoulder, allowing me to see her skin clearly. I lean my head towards her right side, but the light is blocked.

"I see the clothes fit you… just about" she says, biting her lower lip and letting out a brief low laugh as she tilts her head down, giggling into her chest.

I laugh through my smile and pinch at her arm.

"Stop distracting me, Miss Harper" I say.

Without even thinking, I place my hands on her waist and move her with me until she's under the light.

I sit on the bed so I'm closer to her in height, and my head is able to line up better to her neck and collarbone.

I look up at her and our eyes meet.

"I'm so sorry. I did that without thinking. I should've asked you to walk over to the light–."

She interrupts me by placing a finger to my lips gently.

"It's fine Quin. I've told you I trust you".

She moves her finger across my jaw and settles It back by her side. I place my bandaged hand at the nape of her neck to steady her whilst I check her collarbone thoroughly for any remnants of glass.

As I search for any shards, I notice her breathing getting heavier.

I brush away anything lingering on her skin and bring my head back up so that we're face to face. My hand stays at the back of her neck. I can't explain why.

We look at each other for a short while in silence.

Her eyes are telling me she's still feeling guilty.

She reaches my bandaged hand and pulls it from her neck and into her palms. She examines it before placing it against her chest as though she wants to heal me. Little does she know; she's doing exactly that by just existing.

"I'm sorry you ended up injured… again. You'd have been fine if I'd never asked you to come here –."
I stop her by doing as she did to me. I place my finger across her lips. She closes her eyes, almost leaning into my finger.
I slowly move my finger from her lips and trail it across her jaw before cupping it.
"Like I said, I wouldn't want to be anywhere else".

We stay that way for a short while. Both breathing deeply. It's clear that she can feel the tension between us too. My palm cups her jaw as my large fingers graze her neck.
Her eyes are glowing.
They're like two planets filling a dull space with energy, light and pure beauty and I want them closer to me.
I want her as close to me as possible, but I'm not sure if she wants me too.
I lift my other hand and brush it against hers, before gently resting it on the dip of her waist.
She quietly whimpers as my hand makes contact with her.
Neither of us say a word.
She steps even closer to me, closing the small gap that separates us. We both lean towards one another; my hand still cupping her jaw, guiding her face towards mine.
She places her hand against my neck and uses her fingers to draw circles on my skin as our foreheads and noses meet.
We breathe each other in gently, both trembling slightly. As our lips begin to meet, we both smile.
I'm so ready to have her lips on mine again, but more this time. Deeper and harder.

We make contact briefly. It's soothing, sweet and it's like I can feel the fireworks again from the last time.
Our grips tighten on each other and her hips inch closer between my legs as the clothing around my dick tightens.

But the doorbell rings and startles us both, pulling us out of our trance. *Just. Why?*

We both raise our heads, so our eyes meet, before we let out a hushed laugh, lightly resting our foreheads together again before Lista peels herself away from me.
As she walks away, she looks over her shoulder at me, smiling. Her eyes glistening.

"You look good in those tight clothes" she says, looking me up and *down*.

Whilst she's heading to the door, I let my erection and my body in general calm down. It takes everything in me to not run and grab her again, but I resist. I'd rather whatever it is between us, be on Lista's terms.
When I've composed myself, I walk out of her room and stand against the kitchen doorway. She's deposited the pizzas on the kitchen surface and is now sifting through the cupboards getting cleaning supplies.
I can just picture myself lifting her up onto the kitchen surface, standing between her legs and kissing her from head to toe.

She turns to me and looks down. Her face filled with an embarrassed but joyful smile.

"I kind of forgot that I needed to clean the living room, so I'm going to do that now before I get distracted again" she says as she bites her lip and playfully smiles my way.

We both clear up the broken glass and whiskey from the living room, shake off our clothes in the apartments back garden and finish off building the drawers whilst sharing another drink and eating our pizza.

We continue to flirt but steer clear of discussing what happened between us earlier.

I order a taxi eventually and she follows me to the door to see me out. She leans against the wall closest to the door.

"Here's your clothes. I've popped them in a bag so that the taxi is safe from any left-over glass. I genuinely am so sorry about that Quin. But thank you for such a great evening and for helping me out. It's been fun. I needed it after yesterday" she says.

My phone pings. It's the taxi letting me know it's around the corner.

"Thanks for a great evening Lista. It's been a blast" I say, when a newfound confidence flows through me. I realise I can't just leave it where we ended earlier before we were interrupted.

I move into the space between us and wrap my arm around her waist, placing my other on the wall behind her as I lean forward and press my lips to hers.

She grabs my face gently and runs her fingers through my hair.

Fuck, this is even better than the first time I kissed her. I don't want it to end, but I know I can't let it go any further right now. I'll have to relive this to ease the growing bulge in my pants when I'm home.

We regrettably pull our lips apart, but our foreheads are still touching. She gives me one last peck before our bodies separate and I walk out of her door and into my taxi.

Love, In Balance

On the drive home all I can think about is how my body feels when it's pressed up against hers. How right the world feels when I'm with her. How balance is somehow restored.

Chapter 11

Lista

Playlist: *Turn me on* – Norah Jones

Holy. Shit.

I genuinely don't think I've ever felt so in need of another human being before now. Quin just gave me the best kiss of my life before walking out.

What now? I feel like some sort of romance movie character, but what I'm about to do probably wouldn't feature in the final cut.

I'm left feeling so in need of his body on mine, that I take my self to bed and spend the evening making myself feel the delicious release of sexual tension by using my handy stash of sex toys.

I can't deny that Quin is all my mind comes back to. The way his hand was splayed across my waist, sending shivers across my body. His tongue dancing with mine in a perfect, messy rhythm.

My mind takes me back to standing between his legs nervously earlier as he pulled me into him before the doorbell rudely interrupted us. It's always something isn't it?

Love, In Balance

I imagine what could have happened had the doorbell never rang. He'd have kissed me deeply, drinking me in, before I climb on top of his lap, legs either side of his waist, straddling him. I'd kiss him harder before feeling his erection grow more and more as I move around on his lap. We'd realise what we were doing, come back to reality and then rush to begin again, as we know this is exactly what we both want and need. We'd take each other's tops off before he flips me over onto my back, on the bed, and kisses down my neck, breasts and torso. He'd pull off my joggers and continue kissing down my body.

Before I could finish this imaginary scene, I reach my limit and whimper into the silence of my bedroom, picturing Quin on top of me, kissing my whimper away, before falling into a deep sleep.

I wake up the next day, late morning. Quin has already picked up his car and posted a piece of paper through the letterbox with the cutest message.

"Thanks for a great night. I picked my car up but didn't knock because I knew you needed to rest after this busy weekend. Message if you need me. If not, I'll see you soon. Yes, I could've texted you this, but I thought you'd appreciate a shitty letter more. Quin x"

I don't know how to feel or what to think after last night, other than the fact that there's clearly something growing between Quin and I, and it's becoming harder to ignore as the days go by.

I use this free day to organise my head space, comprehend what happened with Pierce, and take some time to reset

before starting a new week tomorrow.
That's what Sundays are for, right?
I wonder if Quin will act any different around me on campus. I'm also questioning whether anything will even come of this. I'm trying not to get my hopes up, but after last night I'm finding it difficult to forget about the way I feel when he's with me.

How can I expect anything though, when he's told me clearly about what happened during his first year of teaching. He can't jeopardise his job by messing around with *me*, a student. Despite being an adult, this situation still comes with its complications and potential repercussions. Great, self-sabotaging again. But in my minds defence, I think imposter syndrome and anxiety are just trying to protect me from having an even more damaged heart. I just need to relax and go with the flow. Whatever happens, happens. The only way to get through is to get through, after all.

It's Monday. I'm feeling anxious but excited to see Quin after how our night ended on Saturday. We've agreed to have a morning meeting in his office to plan sessions and catch up after our research session. I walk onto campus and see Pierce walking in the distance, so I put my head down and speed walk past him. Sadly, I'm unlucky in my attempts to avoid him.

"Hey you. What have you been up to over the weekend. I didn't get to see you after our little encounter at the social. You ran off and left before I could scoop you up and have a proper catch up" he says, rubbing my arm. I don't look at his face. I just continue looking down.

I'd love to grab his arm and twist it backwards. Watch him squirm. I don't, however, carry it out as I'm rather opposed to being arrested. I settle for dismissing the idea of putting thoughts into action, and instead, allow myself to dream.

"I'm late. I have to go" I say, running off before another word can leave his disgusting mouth.

The annoying thing is, he would be so handsome if his personality were less...prick-ish.

That's the charm though. He lures you into a false sense of security with his large stature, his confident stance, muscles and smile. But as soon as the motherfucker starts talking, you realise you've been conned. He's toxic, degrading and makes me feel sick just being near him.

Out of breath, I get to Quins office and knock the door. I may be anxious to see him, but I'm more eager to escape the potential grasp of Pierce and avoid any triggers. So I'm happily welcoming the idea of an awkward first greeting with Quin.

"Come in…".

I hear most of it, but before he even finished his response, I busted in and shut the door behind me.

"Lista. Is everything ok?" he says, standing up quickly.

He moves to the other side of his desk, closer to me, leaning against it.

"Oh… I'm" I try and get my words out, through the panting.
"I'm fine. I just didn't want to be late. And I was just… avoiding someone in the hallway. It's fine. I'm fine" I say.

"Avoiding someone?" he says concerned, frowning and crossing his large arms.
Damn he looks good.

"Don't worry about it Quin. I'm fine. I'm here now so, all good. Would it be ok if I locked the door?" I ask.
It came out before I could even think about the question to be honest.

"Erm… Sure. Go ahead", he says, clearly confused at my bizarre behaviour and request.
He remains leaning against his desk for a while, looking…
It's best not to think about how good he looks right now.
Highly inappropriate.
We discuss Saturday's research session, leaving out the part where he pushed me against the wall, held my waist with those fucking hands, and kissed me. Or the part where I stripped him of his shirt and touched his bare skin.
We put a few dates in the calendar for our future sessions and overall, the meeting is short, swift and productive.

"We could have our sessions here, if need be, or we can continue in coffee shops or wherever suits us both. Where's good for you?" he asks.

"I'd say coffee shops work well, or here. Maybe we should avoid my place" I say, laughing. *Knowing* I shouldn't have brought it up. *Knowing* that on campus I need my professional hat on.

"I wonder why that is?" he says raising his eyebrows.

"Well, we wouldn't want to get carried away or distracted again would we?" I say.
We're flirting now. This wasn't supposed to happen. But damn it feels good.
He flirts back with me even more and it feels dangerous.
"I mean, distractions can happen anywhere Callista. Even in professional spaces" he says, gesturing to the room around us.
I lose all my will to stop.
"So we're not even safe in coffee shops or… your office?" I ask, flirtatiously, smiling.
"Well Callista, it seems like there could be distractions anywhere we work, so we'll just have to try extra hard to avoid them" he says as he takes a few steps towards me, from where he was leant against his desk. He closes the space between us until we're standing about a foot apart.

"Well Doctor Russell" I say, looking up to him and swallowing nervously "I'll certainly try my best, but it might not be easy".
It's then that he clasps my wrist with his less injured hand, holds my waist with the other and pulls me into him. He turns me around and pushes me against his desk.

I feel a rush through my body, moving lower and lower. How do I feel wet already when he hasn't even touched me.

"It really isn't going to be easy Miss Harper" he says, as he lifts me onto his desk, stands in between my legs and kisses me. I kiss him back, and within seconds, our hands are all over each other.

His hand is up my shirt, feeling my bare skin. Mine are in his hair, pulling it gently. We both moan, breathing heavily. I feel his erection growing as he pushes himself near me, between my legs. We align so perfectly like this. He rubs himself against my lower half as we kiss, and I feel pleasure flow through me.

"The first time I saw you on campus" he says, breathing heavily "when you were angry with me. I wanted to wipe that expression off this fucking beautiful face, stand between these gorgeous legs and do this to you" he says, placing kisses on my neck, my jaw and my puffy lips.

"Fuck Lista. It's hard to be around you" he says laughing and placing our foreheads together. His hands still wandering my body, and his groin pressed into mine. Beautiful heat mixing between both of our bodies.

A phone alarm rings, and Quin lifts his head, laughing and shaking it side to side.

"This seems to happen a lot to us. We need a night with *no* interruptions" he says, hungrily.

He leans over me towards his phone and swipes to turn the alarm off before hovering over me and kissing me.

"This'll have to wait unfortunately Lista. I have lectures to prep for" he says, rolling his eyes before kissing me again.

"Let's make sure to keep this off campus in future maybe" he says, with his hands around my waist.

"Understood" I say with another quick peck of his lips. I hop off his desk, tidy myself up and head towards the door. Before I manage to unlock it, he comes behind me, wrapping his hands around my waist again and kisses my cheek.

I feel perfectly aligned after that. My head is clear, and I feel like for once my differences aren't dictating my life. It's nice to know that someone genuine is hungry for me.

Chapter 12

Quin
Playlist: *Still* – Noah Kahan

I'm flustered after this morning.
In a good way, but also with the onset of nerves. Getting caught doing that could end badly, despite how fucking good it felt.
I don't want to be *that* lecturer. And I'm not.

I met Lista before I even knew she was a student. The age gap is small, and we're both mature adults. It's not like I'm preying on an eighteen-year-old. And let's face it, you can't help who you're connected to.
I just wish it was as easy as it should be to be with Lista without potential issues arising. It would be devastating after everything I've been through to get to this point in my career.

I don't want to take fifty steps back, *again*. And I'd hate for it to impact Lista's career and studies too.

I mentally pack my thoughts away, refocusing them on my work for the rest of the day. I set up my laptop and lecture pieces in my lecture room.
Shortly after, Pierce walks in. The air immediately feels heavier. The energy in the room shifts, and I feel weirdly on edge.

He walks everywhere with this cocky kind of confidence. Not the kind of confidence you *should* embody though.

The kind that exudes threat. The kind that's used to belittle others and make them feel less than you are.

It's intimidating, even to someone of my stature. And I quite easily meet his height and bulkiness.

He's a demeaning bastard and the way he talks to people and looks at people pisses me off. I internally ground myself, giving him the benefit of the doubt. After all, he's merely walked through the door.

"Hey Quin. How's it going?" he says. How lovely of him.

I acknowledge him as I would any other person.

"Afternoon. Not bad. I've just been setting up everything ready for lectures today. Everything ok?".

He walks over to the desk, setting his bag down and appears tense. The original façade fading.

"I didn't catch you much at the faculty social. You were there one minute and gone the next" Pierce says to me. He has something on his mind and he's clearly going to make it known.

"Yeah, I left fairly early" I say. Giving a minimal response.

"I saw you with Lista, and then you left when Drew and the guys showed up. Did something happen between you guys?" he asks. *Aha. And There it is.*

"Oh, no. Lista had a panic attack. Something seemed to have triggered her, and I found her outside in a state.

I knew she needed Drew. Once he and the others got to her and she relaxed more, I left and headed home. I didn't want to intrude whilst she was overwhelmed".

"Right ok… I didn't know. No one mentioned it to me" he says. *Yeah, I fucking wonder why.*

"All I know is that she needed Drew, so I called him. He turned up with the guys. Lista is fine now anyway, which is what matters". *Not that you care…*

"What happened to your hand Quin?".
Jeez, is this twenty questions or something? What's with the inquisition?

"I got cut" I say, offering the simple fact.

"Yeah, no shit. How did it happen?".
I didn't realise he cared about my wellbeing so much… I think sarcastically.

"I was helping Lista build some furniture, and the hammer slipped and smashed the glass that I was holding. It cut my hand. It's fine though".

A few minutes pass as I continue setting up for the day, despite Pierce glaring at me.
He is thinking so intensely, that I feel like I can hear him. And I'm waiting for whatever he's got to verbally throw at me. I can feel it. It's like the tension he's holding onto is emitting from his brain and into the room.

Love, In Balance

"So why were you at Lista's?" he comes out with.
I knew it. I had a feeling he was sniffing around for info.

"Not that I need to explain to you, but we had our study session at hers as she was waiting in for a parcel. I'm not sure why I feel like I'm being interrogated here Pierce" I say bluntly. Feeling the need to stand up for myself.

"Hmph. Studying" he says sarcastically.

I'm suddenly extremely on edge around him. He walks towards me, closing the comfortable space between us, crowding my every senses.
I'm not easily intimidated, but this fucking guy. There's just something about him. The way he invades personal space, just like that day at Drews with Lista.
I make the conscious effort to move backwards, despite there being limited space.

"Listen Quin. I've known Lista for a while longer than you and I know what she needs. I see the way you are with her. Following her and appearing at her rescue when she's struggling. I see your little *schemes*". The fucking nerve on this man.
He continues, although his words are not welcome.
"Becoming her advisor suddenly. Spending more time with her and now you're having your *study dates*" he says condescendingly, using his fingers as quotation marks.
He's such a condescending piece of shit.
I have no idea how he got a job working in education.
He still has the nerve to continue, adding a threat this time.

"Getting a student into bed probably isn't going to look so good for you should it *get out*" he says with a mischievous smile. "And me and Lista have something between us. Everyone knows it, and you of all people aren't going to get in the way. So, stay clear of her, otherwise I'll be making sure the faculty staff know your little fucking games with students. And for good measure I could also mention you being a little *too* involved in her research. You know, I guess she'll find it easier by sleeping her way through academia. I'm sure Professor Peters would be interested in that" he says, finishing his speech off with a rough poke to my shoulder, before promptly walking out of the room.

I'm speechless.

I didn't get a chance to defend myself against Pierce this morning, and since then I've had back-to-back lectures with little room for conversation.
He's been in and out of my lecture theatre throughout the day. It's almost as if he's keeping a check on me.
What he said made no sense. He's fucking sadistic.
I knew he was after Lista. I saw it that day in the car park, and at Drew and Oli's game night too.
What difference would it make, her being with him? He's a member of staff too. These thoughts spiral dangerously in my mind and I'm a mess.

Love, In Balance

I keep slipping up whilst presenting, and things get even worse when Lista joins my afternoon session.

She walks in glowing, as gorgeous as ever. Notebook in hand and a smile plastered on her face as she looks over at me. In that moment, I realise how important her career is to her. I remember the conversation she had with the students at the faculty social. She was so devastated about the comments made by the prospective students about her relationships with members of staff.

She works so hard in this male dominated industry and the last thing she needs is people assuming she is only where she is because of the men in her life. I smile slightly back at her, although it's pained.

I thought things would be ok after this morning, wrapped around Lista, but now I'm not so sure.

Chapter 13

Lista

Playlist: *'Like a fool'* - Kiera Knightley (Begin again) soundtrack

I'm not sure if it's just my overthinking, but Quin seems off. His smile wasn't right when I first walked into the lecture room, and he's rarely looked over at me.

Not that I always expect his eyes on me, but it seems as though he's actively avoiding me. Or it's just me. I'm probably just reading him wrong after what happened between us.

I need to stop assuming the worst. It's often not the case.

I won't lie, whenever I watch him speak, I find myself lost to the sight of his lips moving, imagining them on mine like they were again this morning.

He stutters a few times throughout the start of the lecture, but continues strong, as always. He seems tense. Like he's got something weighing on his mind. I'm hoping it's not me. He's collared a few students who spoke over him, and he's seemingly less forgiving than usual. He's raised his voice and reminded everyone of his rules. I've never seen him like this.

He ends the lesson, and I'm looking forward to catching up. I need to plan my next session with him too, so I'm definitely using that as an excuse to speak to him, despite feeling like It'd be a better idea to leave him be.

"Quin, great session. Can I catch you quickly in a moment?" I ask as people are still getting up and leaving.

He looks strained. Tense. He clenches his fists slightly as he looks up at me briefly before speaking.

"Oh, good afternoon Callista. I don't have much time so could you email me" he says bluntly.

I smile, but he just occupies his hands, and keeps his eyes on his laptop, avoiding making anymore eye contact with mine or *me* in general.

He's not joking or playing around, is he?

"Oh. Sure. It's just about our next study session. Is everything ok? –." he abruptly interrupts me.

"Yes, just email me I said, and we can sort it out. I'm just very busy right now, Callista".

Message taken. And he's *far* from joking around.

"Right...Ok *Doctor Russell*" I say as I swiftly walk out with my head down, embarrassed.

Cue self-doubt.

He's regretting it. He's regretting kissing me. He's realised there are far better choices than me out there.

Why did I get my hopes up? I've done it *again* to myself. Thinking he could look past my issues. *Fucking idiot.*

A tear comes to my eye as I speed walk to my car. I

stumble a few times and the pain ebbs and flows in my residual limb. I find that trauma and stress mess with my body immensely. I use the breathing exercises I've learnt and safely make it to my car. As I'm getting in, I see Pierce on the walkway, looking over at me smiling. It's not a genuine smile. It's the possessive kind. I quickly lock my doors and drive away.

Did someone see what we did?
Has someone said something to Quin? Or maybe he's been asked out by someone, so needs to stop our little... whatever it was. Maybe he just didn't want to speak to me in front of other students.

My thought processes on the drive home are dangerous, and I do all I can to stop the tears from clouding my vision. It's difficult. The dizziness comes in waves, and I'm terrified of crashing. Luckily I'm close to home and occupying my thoughts however I can.

I try to drown out the voices in my head by listening to some Taylor Swift, but honestly, all of her songs are so relevant that they make me want to sing full blast and cry until there's nothing left to release.

The songs from Folklore keep me company, and now my life truly feels like a movie. *Thanks TS.*

In very true Taylor Swift fashion, I spend the rest of the night huddled up with Kitty Edith, every blanket I own, endless cups of decaf tea, my current Elsie Silver read, reruns of New Girl, and heaps of my favourite Chinese takeaway food. I deserve it.

I go through everything that happened in my mind over and over, and realise I'm probably just overwhelmed and confused by the sudden change of Quins behaviour.

I do tend to be quite sensitive to other peoples energy.

I put all this panic down to my struggles with regulating my emotions. It wouldn't be the first time I've taken something from a situation and massively blown it out of proportion. The nervous energy dissipates slightly at the thought of this whole thing just being in my mind.

I hope it's that anyway.

I decide to try and put my mind at ease by reaching out to Quin. Coming to a logical mindset helps hugely when I'm spiralling. I'm also not at all passive aggressive. If there's a problem, let's talk and sort it out.

Lista: *Hey, you seemed off during and after the lecture. I hope you're ok. I'm here if you need me. Are you still on for our study session this week? x*

It takes around 10 minutes for his reply. My stomach twists and turns as I open up the message, desperately hoping for an explanation that will help make sense of things.

Quin: *I'm fine. Hope you're ok. Friday should be ok for the session, after lectures. We'll keep them at Cosy Corner Coffee.*
I shouldn't have done what I did with you, so let's just keep this formal and professional from now on. I'm sorry Lista, I really am.

Ok… So, maybe it's not just my difficulties in regulating my emotions.. Has something happened? Does someone know about us?... Or it's plainly obvious; He's regretting what happened because it's *me*. Silly silly me, thinking he was different. Guys always seem to change their mind when it's to do with me.

My chest constricts and I type out my reply through clouded vision from the tears in my eyes.

Lista: *Oh. Ok. Thanks. That's fine. I get it. I won't bother you now. I know you're busy. Sorry for taking up your time.*

I'm feeling fucking petty. And I'm not fucking sorry about it. The lump in my throat is enough to make me feel choked. I'm angry. I'm fucking angry! I've led myself right into another trap. And now here I am.

I've been lifted into bliss, just to be dropped into the shit. Again. I thought this was going to be something real. I was feeling full of hope, safety, sexual tension, happiness and pure balance. Now I'm in a deep pit. No lights on. No one to wrap their arms around me. Just me. Alone with my most depressing thoughts about how unlovable I am, again.
No mum to call.
No dad to threaten to beat up the guy who hurt me.
No little brother to annoy the shit out of me and make me forget all about things. Just me. Alone.
I can't believe I've been this stupid again to think that someone was genuinely interested in me. *Fool.*
I hit myself in the head, pull intensely at my hair, throw my phone and then realise I can't go back to old ways.

My realisation cuts through my cries.
My body does *not* deserve the harm I could cause myself.

I know that when I feel like this, like there's no hope, I fall into dangerous thought patterns, so I reach for my crisis kit. I spend the evening crying, but not hurting myself, which is a huge thing for me.

I struggled with trichotillomania after the accident. I pulled my hair so much that I ended up with bald patches, which in turn lowered my self-esteem and mood even more. With professional help, I recovered, but I still have tendencies which can be triggered by extreme emotional states, like right now.

So I created a crisis kit, with the help of my therapist to prevent self-injury and find more productive ways to get through a bad time.

I play my crisis playlist, which consists of mindfulness exercises, vestibular exercises, calming music and walk through therapeutic meditations.

I use my elastic bands to fidget with and lightly flick on my wrist when I need it. I also use my tweezers to pluck at my leg hairs. These things help to ground me and help me feel something whilst I struggle to cope with the negative thoughts.

I discovered these techniques during my teen years when I struggled with self-harm.

In this moment, I realise how much I've grown and how far I've come. I smile and wrap my arms around myself, because fuck, I deserve it right now.

I don't attend sessions for the next two days.
I can't face it right now, and the amount I've cried has made me feel drained and unwell.
Despite my exercises, my balance is off, and I can't work

like this. I've told Drew and Professor Peters about my
absence and that I'd be taking a few days to recover.
I have however kept the reason to myself. Otherwise, I'll be
seen as the whiny girl who needs days off when she's sad.
And fuck that. Mental health and wellbeing come before all
else, so everyone else can deal with it or swivel.

Drew demands that he and the guys should come over, but
I lie and tell him I don't want them all to catch anything.

Si and his annoying chemistry knowledge keep worming
their way into my inbox, asking what kind of 'ill' I am and
recommending different medications and remedies.
They'd all disown me if they knew I was lying.
Hell, I'd do the same if they were in this position and didn't
tell me. Drew still doesn't know about what happened with
Pierce either. I'm just terrified that I'd be blamed if I told
anyone about how Pierce is with me.
Speak of the devil.
I get a text pop up on my phone. It is certainly not
welcomed.

Pierce: *Hey babe. Nice to bump into you earlier this week.
Haven't seen you much since the social, and you rudely left
without giving me a kiss goodbye ;)*
*I'm still picturing you in that outfit. I need to fulfil my
promise and get my hands on you some more. Maybe I can
come over later this week x*

Who the fuck does he think he is? And what planet does he
live on. I've made it clear that I'm not ok with these
advances, but he thinks I'm just being shy.

I reply instantly.

Lista: *Pierce, again, I'd really rather you didn't message me things like this. I don't need you to come over so please don't. I'm unwell, but I'm fine.*
I walked out of the social because I was struggling. I felt uncomfortable.

Pierce: *Was it Quin who made you feel uncomfortable? I saw him follow you outside x*

Lista: *No. He was helping me.*
I don't know why I'm defending Quin after what's happened. But here we are.

Pierce: *Well, I'm here to help you babe. You know that x*

I don't reply. How is he so blind to his own harassment against me? He seems to think it's all some sort of flirtatious joke.
And yet he's the only one in on it, but it is *not* a fucking joke to me.
After some well-deserved time spent where it's safest; with myself and Edith, I decide to take the rest of the week off.
 I email Professor Peters again and then decide I need to let Quin know about our session on Friday too.
 Not that he'll be bothered. I just know I can't be dealing with him right now with how I'm feeling. And I need to keep as far away from Pierce as possible until I feel stronger.

Am I isolating myself? Yes, I am.

Is it necessary? In my opinion, yes. I don't feel equipped enough to deal with social interactions other than with my cat right now, and my mental, emotional and physical wellbeing come before all else, so I'm doing what is best by me. Thanks. Bye.

Chapter 14

Quin

Playlist: *'Let her go'* – Passenger

It's been two days since I last saw Lista.
She's been off campus since, and I have every reason to believe that I'm the main cause.
I acted like a fucking dick to her, and I hate myself for it, but one day I hope she'll understand why I'm doing it.
I'm doing it for her.
Even though it's killing me to stay away from her.

She needs to be respected by people without being seen with me. I can't bear the thought of people thinking her achievements are somehow linked to who she knows rather than the incredible work she consistently puts in.

I know there's something between us, but with Pierce threatening to talk shit about Lista, I'd rather deal with my internal pain and give Lista the best chance in her studies and career in STEM.

She deserves the world, and I'll do everything I can behind the scenes to make sure nothing compromises that.

Last night I received an email from Lista, cancelling our study session. It broke me, but I respect her decision.
I just hope I don't get taken from her research.
There's really no reason for me to continue contacting her then. I really can't imagine my life without her now that I've had a taste of life with her in it.

From: Callista.Harper97@hotmail.co.uk
Subject: A quick update.

Quin,

I hope you are well. Sorry to bother you. As you may have heard from Professor Peters, I'm taking this week off, and working from home. I will therefore be cancelling our study session tomorrow - Friday evening. I'm sorry for any inconvenience caused by this or by any of my actions recently.
I will be in touch next week to sort out future study sessions. Alternatively if you wish to no longer be my advisor, do let me know.

Kind regards,

Callista Harper MSc
PhD mechanical engineering student
Lived experience practitioner

She's hurting. It's because of me.
But this is better than the alternative, I keep telling myself.
  It's Thursday, the third day of not seeing her.
Instead of wallowing in self-pity, I'm heading out for a bowling and arcade night with the guys for what they call a *'guys night'*. Despite not feeling the best in myself, I agree to go. Drew, Oli, Reed, Pip and Si seemed to realise that I seem off and invited me to cheer me up. *If only they knew.*
  It's clear that Lista hasn't mentioned any of what's happened to the guys.

Love, In Balance

Otherwise I doubt I'd be getting any invitation to their gatherings. Drew would destroy me if he knew I'd hurt her. I feel like destroying myself.

I've considered not going, but Oli and Drew both insisted it'd be good for me. They know something's up, but I'm not one to spread my business around, especially when it involves Lista, so I've just made up an excuse about feeling under the weather.

They don't prod any further, because they're guys I guess, so I just carry on and try to act like I'm ok, even though I'm really fucking not.

I'm glad it's a guy's night, otherwise I'd have had to decline. Not that there's anything wrong with the usual nights they have. But their gatherings usually involve Callista, and I couldn't just gate crash, when she was there first after all. These are her safe people, and I'm not ruining that for her.

But tonight, I'm safe to be around without making her feel uncomfortable. I realise it will be good to do something to just take my mind off her.

That is until halfway through the night, when she walks in.

We've already garnered some attention from a bridal party in the lane next to us throughout the night.
They keep coming over to us, taking selfies and flirting. Any other guy would be happy with this arrangement, but all I can think about is holding Lista and how her legs were wrapped around my waist the other day on my desk.

We've just started the second game of bowling, and as I take my turn, I hear Drew and the guys talking to someone.

I turn around and make direct eye contact with Lista. *Shit*. At that exact moment, the tall blonde woman from the bridal party slaps me on the arse and they all erupt into laughter.

"Sorry, it was a dare" she says and skips away. *What fantastic timing.* Lista sees the whole thing and looks down at the ground, walking in the opposite direction of where I am. Damn. I have sincerely fucked up *again*.

I join the guys and acknowledge Lista normally so that the others don't realise that something is up. We continue the game, but it comes to a pause when something malfunctions. Despite being engineers, we leave it to the staff to fix and use the malfunction as an excuse to top up drinks, grab snacks, take toilet breaks and have a look around the arcade.

On my way back from the men's room, I notice Lista at an arcade machine alone. Not knowing whether I should or not, I just decide to walk over to her before thinking too much into it.

She notices me and sighs, looking away but acknowledging me by speaking.

"Quin. I didn't even think to ask Drew if you were here when he texted me asking me to come, ok? so yeah. I'm not stalking you. I just thought I'd get out of the house for an hour" she says with a hint of anger.

No wonder.

I cannot and do not blame her for her anger and hostility at all. I'd feel the same if I were in her position. I just wish I could explain it to her without repercussions.

"Callista. That's not why I came over to you. You don't need to explain why you're here. You came to see your friends. It's me who shouldn't be here" I say, clearly with no effect because she still looks completely drained and pissed off.

She doesn't speak straight away; she continues assessing the machine she's at whilst sipping her drink, before looking over at the lanes we were playing on and raising her eyebrows, followed by a huff.

"So, I see you prefer tall, slim, flirty blondes with two full legs. Now I understand" she says, laughing into the air and shaking her head. She continues. "For the record though Quin. *You* kissed *me* back. *You* flirted with *me*, and *you* led *me* on. Sorry I'm not quite your type" she says before going to walk away. Before she does, I grab her hand and pull her back so that she's facing me.

"Lista. That woman's just from the lane beside us. They've been drinking and messing about all night. I'm not interested in her or any of them" I say, anger filling my body. "I'm fucking sorry, ok. I don't mean to be a dick to you. I'm just trying to be professional and do the right thing" I say, almost pleading with her to understand.

"Oh so, what we did was the wrong thing? I see Quin" she says, choking up on the hurt I'm clearly causing her.

"No Lista, that's not what I meant. Look. I'm your professor and people won't understand. I don't want this to impact your work. If people found out –." She interrupts before I can finish what I was going to say.

"I get it Quin. I just thought it might be worth it; you know. It's rare that I find good things in my life. It felt good between us. Yeah, it's complicated, but could've worked out. But it's fine Quin. It doesn't matter now. I get it" she says.

It would've been worth it, but she has no fucking idea what Pierce has done and said. I can't think of a response, so I just sigh as she walks away.

"I'm sorry" I say last minute, but what's done is done.

We spend the rest of the night apart, sharing quick glances at each other. It pains me to be apart from her. I want her next to me, holding my hand and in my arms, but instead I pretend everything's fine and accept what life has handed to me.

Well, what *I've* allowed to happen.

We all leave relatively early since it's a work night. Lista offers those of us who got a cab here, a lift. That includes me, which is surprising, since I'm her least favourite person right now.

We all say our goodbyes before me, Drew and Oli get into Lista's car. She drops Oli and Drew home first and then heads to my place since I live closest to her.

We sit quietly with music playing on low.

The tension between us has lessened, but I still want to just reach over to her and hold her in my arms. Just pretend that all of this shit with Pierce never happened, and we just remain content like we were.

"Thanks for offering me a lift. You really didn't have to. I appreciate it" I say.

She smiles slightly and nods her head slowly, still a pained, tired, broken look on her beautiful face.

"It's no problem. I wasn't going to make you guys pay for taxis when I'm driving, and you live so close".

We sit in comfortable silence again before shortly pulling up to my house.

"Well, thanks. It means a lot".

I'm unsure of what to say next before I leave. It's just Lista and I, in a dark car, outside my house. Without really thinking about my words, I just speak.

"Callista, I really fucking like you" I say, before leaning my head back against the head rest and scrunching my eyes shut briefly.

She takes a deep breath and does the same thing, almost melting into the driver's seat, wrapped in her soft cardigan.

Even in such little light, she looks beautiful.

The rage and intensity of my feelings for her is overwhelming. I'm surprised I'm able to sit still.

I've never wanted someone this much in my entire life.

It's fucking painful being without, when we're this close to each other. I want to pull her onto my lap, carry her up to my room and show her what she means to me.

But I just sit here.

"Quin. I really like you too, but there's always a *but* isn't there. Like you said, you're my professor and people won't understand, so let's just leave it at that before this gets any worse".

I reach my hand over and place it on hers before getting out of the car, saying nothing.

Trigger warning – Sexual assault

Chapter 15

Lista

Playlist: *Human* – Christina Perri

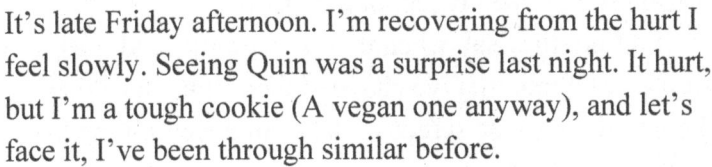

It's late Friday afternoon. I'm recovering from the hurt I feel slowly. Seeing Quin was a surprise last night. It hurt, but I'm a tough cookie (A vegan one anyway), and let's face it, I've been through similar before.
No, I've been through much worse and gotten through it. I can do this.

When the person I was last dating decided I wasn't good enough for him and ghosted me for a while before telling me straight, I fell hard.
Every time I looked in the mirror, I hated what I saw, because I saw myself the way he saw me; Not good enough. Unworthy of his love, and not like the other girls he deemed beautiful.

I lost weight because I couldn't eat.
I was devastated that my biggest fears had come true. I was convinced it would keep happening because I wasn't slim, toned, super fit, bleach blonde, and that I have imperfections.

Love, In Balance

But then I fucking woke up one day and changed the narrative. He wasn't good enough for *me*.
He didn't deserve *me*, and one day someone will come along and love me for exactly who I am; A petite, curvy nerd who is just as beautiful as any model on any magazine cover.

I am beautiful in my own way. Just because I don't look like societies idea of perfection, doesn't mean that I'm not.

I say, *society, you are fucking wrong bab.*
That's why this time, I'm not letting myself be the blame. I've been *'the mistake'* before with men. They like the idea of getting to know me and then getting to know my bed, until they realise my body is different. It's all fun and flirting until they see my leg, or lack thereof.

'Oh, it's fine' they say when they're with me, and then ghost me or tell me they've changed their mind once they get behind their phone screens. They can never tell me to my face though. They only ever gain the courage when there's a keyboard in front of them.
Fucking keyboard warriors.

Quin clearly thought twice after kissing me the other night. His problem.

I've just gotten out of the loveliest bubble bath and finished putting my prosthetic back on when the doorbell rings.
I quickly get my robe on before running to the door, thanking my stars that I decided to put my leg back on this evening, otherwise whoever's at the door may have left by the time I get there.

It's probably just a delivery, but since I don't have a porch, or safe place, I always try to get to the door.

I should probably invest in a ring doorbell.

That's exactly what I think when I open my door. It's Pierce. I now kind of wish I didn't have my prosthetic on, so that I could've taken a long time, and he would've kindly fucked off.

"Pierce, hi. It's not a good time" I say, as I close the door over, but he catches it with his foot. He pushes it open.

"Hey sweet, I was just checking in on you. I haven't seen you since the social. I've been thinking about you" he says, putting a hand on my arm. I flinch backwards.

"Pierce, It's not necessary honestly. I'm fine. I was just in the bath, so –." he interrupts, walking in and closing the door behind him.

"Ooo in the bath ay? Lucky me, seeing you in your robe with nothing underneath" he says with a raised eyebrow.
Fucking creep. He makes me feel sick.

I walk away over to my phone, internally panicking.

I don't feel safe. Especially after what happened at the faculty social, and the nature of the text messages he's been sending. Whilst I doubt he'd do anything to hurt me in my own home, I can't rely on hope alone here. SSDGM. And after what happened before, I feel better to put something in place. So, I decide to do something I've never done; I text Drew *the code*. I can only hope he sees it.

Lista: 🖤 🖤 🏠 (Two black hearts and a house = I need help. It's urgent. I'm at home)

"Look Pierce, I'm not feeling up for socialising right now. I'm taking some time for myself".

"Lista, I'm just checking in. I care about you. I wanted to be here for you." he says, sure of himself.
As if he has a conscience.
He walks towards me, and I step back into the wall. Nowhere else to go. I decide to tell Pierce straight.

"Pierce, I don't feel ok with you being here. I left the social because you made me feel uncomfortable by what you said to me. I felt disgusted in myself for what I was wearing. So please leave". He crowds me, leaving little space between us.

"Lista. I'm sorry but I think you're overexaggerating".
Nothing like a little bit of gaslighting is there?

"I was just playing around and giving you a compliment. You know what I'm like. Plus, we've got this little thing between us haven't we, sweet? I'm sorry for upsetting you". He says the last part with some sincerity, whilst leaning towards me and wrapping his arms around me for a hug.
He briefly makes me feel bad for saying those things and I start to question whether I'm the one taking it the wrong way… that is why I didn't tell anyone how I felt, after all, isn't it?

"Pierce, it's fine".

But I realise that actually, *no*, it is not fine. But right now, more than anything, I just want him to leave.

I stand awkwardly but provide a quick and swift pat to his back in a friendly manner. That's when he brings his hands to meet my waist as he plants his face in my neck and breaths against my skin. I shiver and fidget rigidly.
I try to pull away but his grasp on me is strong. He's taller and stronger than me, so trying to wriggle out of his hold is difficult.
He whispers into my ear and tears fill my eyes.

"Do you know how long I've wanted you. How much I've wanted my hands on you" he says possessively.

"Pierce, please let me go. This isn't right" I say shakily.

"Babe, it's just me and you here right now".
Yeah, fucking tell me about it.
"Don't fight it. You know you want it".
I hate this. I wish I could disappear. I try harder to move. He just continues talking and touching me.
"We can do whatever we want to do, like *last time*" he says and then kisses and nips at my neck with force.
I yelp, tears filling my eyes to the brim, beginning to overflow.
My neck stings from where he nipped me, and I feel dirty. Him reminding me of last time makes me want to vomit. I'm scared. No. Fucking terrified.

"Pierce, I don't want to do anything. I want you to leave. Please Pierce". I plead with him.

Love, In Balance

"You said *that* last time. Always playing hard to get" he persists, laughing under his breath and explaining that I'm in denial and that I know how we're meant to be together.

"Since the first day you came to the university all those years ago, I clocked you. The things I've wanted to do to you" he says with a roughness to his voice.

He pushes me further back against the wall, so that I'm pinned in place and starts running his hands through the gap in my robe, loosening it, exposing my body.
I squirm beneath his touch, and he tightens his grip. I can feel his nails scratching against my skin.

"Pierce, let me go right now. I don't want this, and I don't want to be with you, so please" I say, pushing my hands against his chest so that I can get away, but he grabs my hands and pushes them up against the wall above my head. I start to cry, continuing to plead with him to let me go.

I think I hear the sound of someone outside the door and the rattle of keys, but with him crowding my every sense, focusing on much else is near impossible.

"Stop resisting babe. You know you've dreamt of this. I'll give you more than last time. Plus, Lista, do you really think anyone else will be as understanding about your body as I am. Look at how many guys have ditched you because of your leg. Count yourself lucky that I see past it".

He's kissing my neck again and making his way up to my lips. He bites my bottom lip, and I move my head to the side. He continues trying any way he can.

In that moment, I believe him about my leg and how other guys see me, and I feel lost.

I can't escape his grip no matter how hard I push against it. I'm alone.

I close my eyes and try to go into a different world in my mind, to numb myself to what's happening like I did last time, knowing I can't get away.

But Pierce has moved his mouth over my breasts, nipping at my flesh aggressively, and I cry louder, begging him to stop.

That's when I hear footsteps getting closer, louder and more hurried.

I forgot I messaged Drew the code. I'm praying it's him I hear, using the key he has for my apartment.

It is. He walks around the corner and sees us, briefly making eye contact with me, before realising what is happening. He probably heard my cries and Pierces voice before all else.

His expression changes. An anger crosses his face that I've never seen before. He runs towards where Pierce has pinned me against the wall and grabs him by the shirt, pulling him backwards, peeling him off me.

I cry, gathering my robe around me to cover my body and wrap it between my legs before sliding down the wall onto the floor, tucking my knees into my chest, hugging them.

I plant my head into my legs to shield my eyes from Pierce. I try to zone out again, but the background noise is loud. I place my hands over my ears.

Everything around me is muffled and the dizziness finds me, making me feel like the room is spinning around me. I struggle to keep balanced, despite being sat on the floor and against the wall.

Love, In Balance

I hear Drew raising his voice and cry at the sudden relief that *someone* is on my side.

"How fucking dare you lay a hand on her. And you didn't think to stop when she told you to. When she said *no*. When she started fucking crying. No. You're a fucking monster Pierce. How could you do this to her? She's meant to be your friend! And what the fuck did you mean by *last time?*" *Drew says. Gritting his teeth.*

Pierces response comes next, but I tighten my grip around my ears so that I don't hear his voice. What if he accuses me of wanting this. What if Drew believes him. What if I *am* to blame.

Drew speaks again.

"It's harassment Pierce. She said *no* and you continued. You took advantage of her and exposed her in her own fucking home. Now get. out. Before I fucking throw you out. And if you ever even look at her again, you'll know about it. She is one of the most important things in the world to me, and I'd soon destroy you before letting you touch another hair on her head. Don't message her. Don't look at her. Don't speak to her. Understood? Now get out".

I hear Drews voice near me and feel a warm glow around me before feeling a light pressure around my arms. I lift my head out of my knees.

Drew has enveloped me in a hug. We come face to face, and in that moment, I realise I'm safe. He chose me. Not Pierce.

"Drew… This has been going on for a long time. I'm so sorry" I say, sobbing. I have no idea what else to do, but just tell him as it is.

"Lista, what do you mean? Why haven't you said anything?".

I reach over to grab my phone from the side table, pull up the message thread from Pierce and let him read it. He holds my phone in one hand and covers his mouth with the other.

"Lista, why didn't you tell me this was going on? He didn't touch you before, did he?" he asks. Concern rushes over his features.

My face falls and I burst into tears further at his question.

I manage to speak in sentences, despite fluctuating between hiccupping and crying.

"He was the reason I had a panic attack at the faculty social. He approached me and made me feel disgusting because of the things he said about my outfit". My lip begins to tremble as I hesitate to go on, but Drew gently lays his hand on my back, giving me the strength to continue.

"He touched me, squeezed my bum and…pushed his lower body against me. He was... hard. I could feel it. He kissed my neck too." I put my palms over my eyes, rub until I see stars and then continue.

"He forced me to kiss him when we went on that trip with the guy's early last year. I was crying, but he continued. He had me cornered. That same night, he snook into my room… I woke up early hours in the morning because… he had his fingers inside of me... I didn't want to tell you because he's your friend. I thought you'd think he was just joking around or that it was consensual. I didn't want to seem like I was blowing the situation out of proportion.

He kept on saying that he was joking and when I'd react, he'd tell me I was overexaggerating. I assumed everyone else would think the same".

Drews looks straight at me, eyes filled with tears, some falling down his face. He holds me again and whispers in my ear "I'm so sorry. I'm here now and I'll never let this happen again".

"Let's get you into something more comfortable Lista". Drew moves a step back and helps me onto my feet before guiding me into my room. He hands me some soft loungewear before walking away, closing the door over.

"I'm making hot chocolate. Come out when you're ready" he says, making me smile despite how I'm feeling.
I love him so much and I'm so grateful to have him in my life. I can see why Flic may very well be in love with him, even if *she* doesn't even know it yet.

He's the most beautiful soul, and I get to call him my best friend. My eyes fill with tears again, but they're warmer and full of happiness and contentment. I know that I'm safe, and I can't quite explain the impact it has on my body. It's like I've unclenched my muscles for the first time in years. I've felt so lonely for so long. But now I *know* I have people in my corner. I can't help but want to hug the others and tell them how much I appreciate them.

Once I've gotten changed and taken my time to process what's happened, I spend the rest of the evening drinking hot chocolate and watching reruns of New Girl with Drew and Flic.

He called her over whilst I was changing. I'm unsure of whether he called her for moral support for himself, or for me, but either way, it's perfect.

Drew told the group what had happened, and I've never felt so protected in my entire life. They all messaged me, letting me know they were just a text away. Drew mentioned that Si actually shed a tear and almost punched something when he was told what had happened. Apparently he only settled when Drew assured him multiple times that I was ok and relatively unharmed. *That sweet son of a bitch.*

Flic cried with me when she walked into my flat and we made eye contact. She wrapped me in her arms, and we sat side by side on the sofa before settling down. They both stayed with me to help me feel safer.

It was exactly what I needed.

I couldn't help but think of Quin this whole time still. Him and I, sitting together with blankets and hot chocolate. When Drew held me as I cried, I imagined it was Quin. Even the way Drew and Flic look at each other takes my mind back to Quin. Never mind.

Chapter 16

Lista

Playlist: *It's Ok* – Nightbirde live version

The weekend goes by quickly. I've stayed home, ordered in coffee and cake to treat myself, and I've taken time to heal. Since Drew has been working and couldn't get here until late evening, Si has been around every day to check in with me, ensuring I have the right foods, drink and vitamins. You see, he does have a heart. It's just super deep within and takes a while for an outsider to locate it.

When you do though, he's a keeper. I'm pretty sure he's resisting asking me if he can sleep at the foot of my bed like a guard dog. He really is intense when he cares.

Flic has even come over to have a few evenings of watching films which has been exactly what I've needed.

Drew ordered me a ring doorbell the night that shit went down with Pierce. He installed it the next day and hooked it up to my phone so that I never have to answer the door without knowing who's there.

We've spoken a few times about what happened and I'm still unsure about reporting it to the police and the university.

I want to prevent this from happening to anyone else, but I'm terrified.

I'm scared that people won't believe my side of things and that they'll take his word that it was all consensual.

I can imagine him downplaying it as *just flirting.* So it's a vicious cycle in my mind.

This is the conclusion I keep reaching, so I know that until I'm sure, I need to leave that trail of thought and focus on getting back on my feet. Recovery takes time.

Hell, sometimes it's a never-ending journey. Mental and physical healing isn't done instantly, and I've realised throughout life to be gentle with myself. I don't need to rush. When I'm strong enough, I will do the right thing, and in the back of my mind, I know exactly what that means.

I use the weekend to gather my thoughts and have a mental and physical declutter and organisation. I go through my wardrobe and sort out items to sell, things to give to charity and things that will only benefit from seeing the inside of the bin.

I've photographed my fancier clothes and put them onto Vinted to sell, and Si has driven the bags of unwanted clothes to our local homeless charity to be reused and re-loved.

I've sorted my kitchen and done an order of fresh food, plus I've deep cleaned, and I honestly feel brand new.

For me, decluttering my home helps me clear my mind and reorganise those mental boxes. *100% recommend.*

The next day I aim to go back to campus, but it proves difficult. I wake up and realise it's harder than I thought it would be. The realisation that I'd have to face both Quin and Pierce in lectures, in the hallways and in general. It hit me harder than I'd anticipated and pushed me back a few steps.

I wrote a lengthy email to Professor Peters and explained that something had taken place over the weekend and that I'd be on campus later than expected. His reply is something I hadn't quite expected. I had to read it twice.

From: *Peters.T.L_Engineering@hotmail.com*
Subject: *Re. Return to campus*

Callista,

Regarding your email, I must be fair and treat you the way all tutors are expected to with their students. Therefore, the longer you stay away from campus, I will have to consider taking your absences to higher ups. The university does not tolerate prolonged absences, other than in exceptional circumstances. If you wish to discuss this any further, you will need to come onto campus.

Dr Lance T Peters
Head of Engineering

I'm absolutely fuming about this response. I have no idea who has shit in his cereal, but to take it out on me is unacceptable. Not only has he failed to even ask about my circumstances and reasons, but he's making me feel like I'm burdening him.

  I'd understand if this was a common occurrence from me, but I've rarely had any time off since I began my journey in higher STEM education almost ten years ago.

I've maybe missed a few hours across the span of a term whilst having my prosthetic changed or when having physio, but the majority of the time, I plan it so that my days at Uni aren't impacted.

I've always been a high achiever with perfect punctuality and near perfect attendance, and yet the one time I've been through hell and back and in need of some time away, I'm penalised for it. *Fucking guy.*

Within an hour, I'm dressed, with some war paint on (makeup, to those who need that narrative reworded), and I'm in my car on my way to the university.

His email was the kick up the arse my mind needed, to give me the 'fuck you' energy to face my fears and kick some ass. Main character energy right there. That's what's getting me through this. Although I do still want to stay in the comfort of my blankets and shed a few tears whilst stuffing my face with Lilah's vegan treats from Cosy Corner Coffee.

I arrive on campus and head straight to Peters' office. I knock, and despite not hearing him call out, open the door and walk in.

"Oh, hi Callista. I didn't expect you back so soon", he says in greeting.

"Oh, did you not? Because your email wasn't as understanding as you're sounding right now. So, I thought I'd come in and discuss this face to face as you required. And before you say anything, I'm here now and I'm planning on staying, despite my internal struggles after the nightmare I had over the weekend. Thanks for asking by the way. So no need for the big discussion about my circumstances. I do however need to be removed from all lectures that Professor Pierce will be attending. That is all I need from you and then I won't bother you any further". As soon as I stop talking, I'm in both shock and awe at myself. *Yes. Bitch.*

He looks up from his desk after examining something on his computer and looks like I've just offended him dearly.

"Callista, I don't appreciate your tone. And whatever has happened between you and Doctor Pierce doesn't mean I can just dismiss you from classes he's in. Just because you may have had a little fallout doesn't warrant you to avoid him in educational settings –." I interrupt him.

"Oh, Professor, I can assure that a 'little fallout' doesn't quite capture my situation. I would also like to say that regardless of whether I'm removed from the classes he attends or not, I will *not* be in them".

"Well, Callista, if all students were just able to choose which classes they did and didn't attend when they please, because of silly fallouts, we'd be in a bit of a pickle wouldn't we? So, if you insist on missing classes, I'm afraid I will have to report you to the higher ups and have your education with us reviewed."

The fucking cheek of this man.
He has still failed to ask me what happened but continues as if I'm a child. At that moment, I do in fact, lose my shit.

"Well for your information, professor, over the last two weeks I have been sexually harassed and assaulted on two separate occasions by Doctor Pierce. Once at the faculty social, hence my absence last week, and once on Friday evening, in *my* home, after he turned up and forced his way in uninvited. *This*" I say tilting my head and pulling my top collar down "is from him biting my neck, whilst pushing me against the wall. And this" I say lifting my top slightly "is just one of the marks he left on my abdomen from his hands gripping me as I tried to get him off me. So *no*, I will not be attending sessions when he is present, and if you'd like to report me, be my guest, but I will fight my case. If you deem my reasons *silly* or *childish* then I'm sure higher ups would like to know how little you consider harassment to be an issue. Oh, and I don't appreciate *your* tone or lack of care, not even attempting to ask me what had happened before penalising me and assuming my situation was like that of a primary school child. Now, I'm going to a study room and working on my research, alone. And I *will* be making a case against Pierce as soon as I feel able to. Thank you for your time."

He doesn't say anything as I walk out.
I run, keeping my head down, to my study room and lock the door behind me as I burst into tears.

There's a knock at the door.
I freeze, blood rushing through my body and I'm terrified that it's Pierce. I turn, move the blind slightly to the side and see someone through the narrow window in the door. It's Quin.
I open the door and instantly feel relieved.

"Quin, it's not a great time" I say as I open the door.

"Callista, what's wrong?" he says, full of genuine

concern. He looks like he hasn't slept.

"Quin, in the nicest way possible, does it really matter to you?" I say whilst looking down. "I just needed to be away from classrooms and lecture theatres right now. So, I'm studying in my own space instead if that's ok. Don't worry Quin. I'm fine".

He looks around and then looks down, reaching for my hand as he steps slightly inside the room where the door is ajar.
"Lista, I'm sorry, ok. I can't explain at the moment, but I just saw you rush in here upset and I wanted to make sure everything was ok" he says, brushing his thumb against my hand as he holds it gently. I want to be wrapped up in his arms more than anything. His presence stops the world from spinning. He's the calm to my storm.

"Quin. *Nothing* is ok right now… but it will be. Don't worry about me. Just get on with your day. I'll be fine" I say as he lets my hand go and steps out of the doorway.

"I won't stop worrying, but I trust you and respect your wishes. Just please… please be ok" he says pleadingly as he walks away. But after only a few steps, he turns back.

"Lista… One day I'll be able to tell you why…" he stops, almost as if he's rethinking what he's trying to say "Just trust me when I say that I'm not ok either, because I've been away from you, but I'm doing it *for* you. I… *Fuck*, I just can't explain it right now. Just please be ok" he

finishes speaking, and then walks away this time with his head down, shaking.
I'm so confused. I thought he regretted kissing me, but that encounter was far more…intimate than I'd expect.

I spend the rest of the day studying, researching and finding ways to fill the void that is now my mind. I'm a bundle of confusion, anxiety, and what-the-fuckery, to put it one way. After getting some work done and managing to briefly forget my current kerfuffle, I head home. I even make a draft email to send out in order to get a case made against Pierce. It's far from finished, but it's a start, and that's what matters. The hardest part is starting something. The rest will follow.
I can only thank Professor Peters for activating 'get shit done and fight back' Lista. She's *boss*.

Chapter 17

Quin
Playlist: *SORRY* – Macklemore and Livingston

Why did I take her hand in mine? Anyone could have seen it. Pierce could've seen.
I just can't help myself. There's something about her that pulls me to her, and when I saw her run into the study room, upset, I had to make sure she was ok.
It's understandable that she'd rather not talk to me, but I really hope this whole upset isn't caused by me.
And I hope one day I can tell her exactly why I've done what I've done.

When I head back to my lecture room, Pierce is there. I ignore him, as I've been doing since he threatened me. Today he seems reserved though. He offers no further threats, thankfully and briefly speaks, asking me random questions.

"Seen Lista lately?" he says, looking like he's trying to act normal.

"Why would I Pierce? I'm not one to try and jeopardise her career. So, *no* I haven't. I merely passed by her not long ago but that's about it. Is that acceptable?" I say, pissed off and wanting him to leave me the hell alone.

"She's on campus? Right now?" he asks, almost in a mild panic.

"She was recently but I'm not sure if she left. Why?". I'm becoming more suspicious of him now.

He avoids my questioning and continues to question me.
"How about Drew? Have you spoken to him today? Or the guys?" he says, nervously, looking around.

Am I missing something?
"No Pierce I haven't. Now if you don't mind, I'd prefer to go back to setting up my last few sessions in peace. If you're so worried about Drew and Lista, go and speak to them yourself". *He takes the hint.*

My day is mundane, and I just about manage to get through. Everywhere I look, I see the void that Lista usually fills with her presence. I somehow pull myself together and push through, despite feel empty and confused by how everyone around me is acting.

After my second to last lesson, Drew comes in to ask for something. He clocks Pierce, who was present during my session, and his face and fists harden.

He approaches me, and we discuss what he needs. It's a pleasant surprise that he's still speaking to me. I guess Lista hasn't spoken to him about us yet.

I do however notice and find it odd that the entire time he's in my room, he ignores Pierce. Quite obviously too. I can feel the tension between them and so many questions are circling my already tired and confused mind.

Love, In Balance

"Thanks Quin. Have a good one mate" Drew says before leaving. I decide not to comment on the obvious confusion I'm feeling and leave Pierce to stew in whatever he is experiencing right now. Fuck this guy.

"Thanks Drew. And you" I say, before he leaves.

Throughout my entire session, I'm running through everything I've experienced today and feel like I'm missing something. Like everyone got the memo, but me.

When I head out to leave, I notice Lista walking through the car-park and decide to stand by the door and make sure she leaves safely before I walk to my car.
She sees me and offers me a brief wave and sad smile as she drives away. I wave back, content that she's safe. It's the least I can do.

As I'm approaching my car, Drew runs over to me, panting from running.

"Hey Drew. Everything ok? Callista just left. You missed her by mere seconds. I watched, just to make sure she got to her car safely" I say, filling in the silence whilst he catches his breath.

"Thanks Man. I didn't realise she was on campus until an hour ago. I tried to rush to get here to walk her to her car but I'm too late, clearly. Thanks for watching out for her".

"Oh, I mean, no worries. I'll always look out for her. If I see her going to her car, I make sure she gets to it safely before I go. I mean, I haven't seen her since she took some time off, but then I noticed her rushing to the study room today and I checked in to make sure everything was ok. So yeah. *Is* everything ok Drew?" I ask genuinely concerned and confused about...well, everything.

"Quin. Has Lista not spoken to you since the weekend…?" he asks wide eyed.

"I haven't spoken to her since last Monday. We…" I stop, considering my next words carefully. "We kissed Drew. *Again.* I couldn't help myself. We had our research session at her house whilst she waited in for a delivery and one thing led to another. I was stoked, but then I came onto campus last week and… something happened so I was forced to distance myself from her. I think I've fucked up. She hates me. I don't want her to think I regret what happened, but I had no choice. I *have* no choice. It's all for her. I'm doing this for her".

Drew looks ultimately confused by what I've just said, and I'm genuinely scared that I'm about to receive a punch to the nose. All in all, I probably deserve it.
"Wait, hold up. Why did you make sure she got to her car safely?" Drew asks.

After everything I've just told him, that's all he wants to know.
"Because first of all, I care about her" I say, rubbing my hand over my face as if I'll find some courage by doing so "and… I know this sounds ridiculous but a while ago, when we first become reacquainted after New Year's, I was walking to my car, and I noticed Lista heading to hers too

in front of me. Pierce followed her and startled her. Although I couldn't hear, Lista seemed uncomfortable whilst he was talking to her. Similar things happened that night at yours. I wasn't sure if Lista told you or not. I didn't think it was my place to say, and I know Pierce is your mate, so –" He interrupts.

"Oh, he is no fucking mate of mine. Not after last weekend. And the fact that you have watched out for her without even knowing what's happened". He shakes his head and takes a huge breath in before exhaling slowly. Anger floods his features.

Ok now I'm even more confused.
"Drew, what's going on? Is Lista *ok*?" I ask as my breathing changes, and I start to feel panic. I ask him outright, so I can get to the bottom of whatever the hell is going on, because I'm tense all of a sudden and my gut tells me something is very wrong.
What happens next takes my body to a different phase of existence to my mind.

"Quin. I need you to stay calm mate" he says to me, resting his hand on my shoulder. "Pierce sexually assaulted Lista on Friday night. He turned up to her flat and entered uninvited before forcing himself on her. She managed to text me our emergency code when he arrived because she didn't feel safe. I let myself in and saw him pinning her against the wall, restraining her and... touching her. I got there before he could do anything else, thankfully. He's left marks and she's really struggling because of it. Apparently, this isn't the first time…" he says, looking down. His hand still on my shoulder.

I'm speechless. I frown, not knowing what to say or do. A feeling of anger fills my body. *This is my fault.*
 "It's my fault" I mumble. "I was meant to see her on Friday, but she cancelled because of how I acted towards her. This never would have happened if –".

I look up and see Pierce in the distance leaving the campus building, heading into the car park. The next chain of events I seem to watch from outside of my own body.
 I shrug off Drews grip on my shoulder and walk past him without saying a word, picking up my pace the closer I get to Pierce, before grabbing him by the front of his coat and slamming him against the wall.
 "Is this how you like it, ay Pierce? Being pinned against the wall? How fucking dare you lay a finger on Callista. You piece of shit! You pushed me away from her with your manipulative threats and then went in for the kill, didn't you? Do you like taking advantage of your students. Using them for your own pleasure. I've seen how you've objectified her, followed her around. Was it you that caused her to flee the faculty social? Is that why you threatened me to stay away from her. So you could pounce and harass her, keep her all for yourself?" I point into his chest with force, "*You* best be the one to stay away from her from now on. I fucking swear Pierce. Don't even look at her. Or any one for that matter. You're a fucking predator. Has Lista not been through enough. You asshole!".
 Tears fill my eyes and my voice trembles.

All I can think about is how hurt Lista is. All of this, she has been carrying, because of this prick. I go to swing for him, but Drew grabs my wrist and my other arm and pulls me away.

I cry out a grunt and punch the brick wall to release this pent-up anger. Not hard enough to break anything, but enough to leave marks. And yes, it was the hand that's still recovering from the last injury.

Drew pulls me towards him, to walk me back to the car and brings me back to reality.

The black clouds around my vision come back and I notice Professor Peters and a few students around us, watching. Pierce shakes off the creases I've left from my fist wrapping around his shirt and walks off swiftly to his car. I turn to Drew, and he puts his hand on my shoulder.

"I didn't realise how you felt about her Quin. I assume she doesn't know that Pierce is the reason for you keeping your distance. If so, I think you need to tell her mate."

After Drew sees me to my car and settles me down from my rather explosive moment, he heads over to de-escalate the situation with onlookers, before heading to his car.

He leaves me with my own thoughts. The first thing that crosses my mind is Lista. I *need* to see her and make sure she's ok. I need to explain myself. But most importantly, I just need to know she's safe. I need her. I don't care what Pierce threatened to do. I'm well and truly done with putting my life and happiness on hold because of other people's fucking rules.

Chapter 18

Lista

Playlist: *Balance* – Lucy Spraggan

I get home and wrap myself in cosy blankets, shielding myself from the world. I cuddle Kitty Edith and accept lots of nose kisses. She really does heal my fractured soul.

I open my phone and message Drew, telling him about everything that happened today with Professor Peters. I also send a picture of myself and kitty Edith.

I make the decision to head onto campus tomorrow to face my fears and continue being the badass that I am, but the anxiety it brings is immense.

So tonight will involve chocolate ice cream, hot chocolate (*Weird combination. I'm aware*) and some easy-going TV. You guessed it! New Girl...*again*.

People don't seem to understand my need for the nostalgia, routine, repetition and lack of risk of disappointment that rewatching shows or films brings me. So, suck it people! This is my life, and I can watch the same episodes twenty-five point five times all I like. *Ok?* Yeah, that's what I thought.

Alongside the noise of my inner dialogue comes the doorbell, followed by a man's voice, muffled by the door and walls separating us. I can just about hear the words being said.

"Lista. It's me, Quin. If you'd like me to go, please just say, but". I unwrap the blanket from myself, revealing just my cosy pyjamas. I walk over to my front door, opening it before he can say anymore. He continues when we're face to face.

"Lista, I understand if you don't want me here, but I need to know that you're safe".

I'm glad to see him. I feel a warmth come over me. He's never seen me like...*this*. And yet he makes no changes to the way he addresses me.

"Quin, it's ok. You can come in" I say softly with a gentle smile. He comes in and I close the door behind us.
He walks us both over to the couch, hand on the base of my spine, ensuring I'm sat down and comfortable.

Quin then immediately speaks, almost panicking to get his point across.

"Lista, I never wanted to ignore you… He fucking threatened me. He told me he'd out you as sleeping with a professor to get to where you've come in your career.
I couldn't bear the thought of you being hurt or degraded. I did it so he *couldn't* hurt you, and yet he fucking has. I'm so sorry for letting you down. I wanted to keep you safe and all I've done is caused shit for you".

He steps towards me gently, leaning down and brushing his hand across the bruise on my neck.

"Are you hurt? Did he fucking hurt you?" he says as his eyes fill with tears. He looks down, clearly trying to hold back his emotions.

I stand up from the sofa, towards him and place my hand against his face, feeling the slight stubble against my palm. He's warm and slightly sweaty, as though he's been running. I've never seen him like this.
Cool, calm, collected Quin, is not so... cool, calm or collected. Quite the opposite.

I can't believe that Pierce has caused so much damage, not only to me, but to Quin as well. *He's* the reason Quin has been distant with me.
I feel anger boil within me, but I know that everything is out now, and the most important thing is that Quin is here, with me.

"I'm ok Quin. Better now that you're here".
He places his hand over mine on his face.

"I never wanted to hurt you Lista. I never meant to kiss you and then just ignore you. I swear. I didn't see a way out. No matter what I did, it would end up hurting you, but I know how much your career in STEM means to you and I could never fuck it up for you by risking people knowing about us. I should've just told you about what that prick had said, but I didn't want you to worry. So I decided to distance myself instead, like a fucking idiot. You are worth so much more than what has been done to you. As soon as Drew told me and I dealt with Pierce, I came straight here" he says, lifting his hand slightly and peering down at it. I get even closer to him. His hand is scratched and swollen.

"Quin. Just…stop" I say gently, rubbing over the sore parts of his hand. Not ignoring what most likely could have happened, but not focusing on it either. That's so far from important right now.

"We're here. In my home, together. I'm ok. So, stop beating yourself up. The fact that you've come here genuinely to check on me tells me how much you care. You've never made me feel unsafe, the entire time I've known you, and you always look out for me, regardless of how you feel. Yes, it broke me when you acted like nothing happened between us, but now I know why, and I understand why you did what you did. You mean a lot to me, so thank you for being in my life" I say as I tip toe to press my lips against his briefly, steadying myself by placing my hands against his chest.

I come back to stand normally, so small against his large frame. I feel like my body has turned to liquid just from the brief touch of his lips against mine.

The small amount of contact seems to have grounded him. His eyes remain shut. Lingering for long seconds, taking a deep sigh of relief before lowering his raised, tense shoulders.

He opens his eyes and looks straight into my own, seemingly peering into my soul.

"Lista" he says as he closes the space between us, placing his hands on my waist, helping me find the perfect balance as I stand here exhausted after the last few weeks. "I know this may not be the right time, and please tell me if you need space or time, or if you just want me to leave. But from the moment I met you on New Year's Eve, I wanted you. Everything about you pulled me to you, and when I found you again after feeling like I'd lost the chance with you forever, I felt it so much stronger. I will always be here; however you want that to look, but you need to know that I want you. All of you. And if you feel the same, I'm willing to get through whatever problems come our way, together".

I feel my eyes become watery, and as tears flow down my face, I lean in and press my lips to his again, this time with the addition of both of my arms wrapped around his neck, meeting at the back, feeling his soft hair on my palms. His arms wrapped around my waist, pulling me closer than we've been before, as our tongues entwine passionately.

We each smile into the kiss, gripping each other tighter, not wanting an inch of space to be lost between us. It feels so right, and I want more of him, but he pulls back, looking at my face closely.

"How do you feel Lista?" he says.

"Quin, right now I'm the most content I've been in a long time. Despite everything that's happened, now that I'm in your arms, I feel safe again".

He kisses my forehead lightly, pulling me closer to him.
"I'm…I just don't want to do anything to you to make you feel…uncomfortable or triggered after what you've been through recently. So, if you there's anything I do that would do that, you have to tell me" he says, so gently. I can't believe I have this man in my arms again after everything.
I take a deep breath in.

"Quin. Nothing you do could make me uncomfortable, because it's you. Yes, I've been hurt, but when it's you, touching me, kissing me, and holding me, I feel like everything is ok".

I melt into his chest once again because although I've been scarred by what Pierce did, when I'm with Quin, I feel at ease, safe and balanced. The furthest away from a trigger. More like a glimmer.

After what feels like a lifetime lost happily, buried in his chest, with his arms wrapped around me, I tip toe again, our lips meeting. I kiss the line of his jaw until I reach his ear where I needlingly whisper "I want you".

Chapter 19

Lista

Playlist: *All I wanna do is make love to you* - Halestorm

The moment I whisper in his ear, he scoops me up in his arms and carries me into my room, gently asking if it's ok. I of course, say yes.
He sits on the edge of my bed, still holding me with my legs around his waist. After a few brief kisses, he mumbles into my lips.

"This is where I wanted you last time, before we were rudely interrupted" he says, charmingly. We both laugh.

Our bodies meet and the sweet tension that has built up throughout our time together is dissipating around us in beautiful waves.
Our tongues meet, our hands are all over each other, and it's the release we both needed after this shitshow of events.

I slowly unbutton his shirt, and he gives me time and space to do what I need, when I feel right. But as gentle as he is, and as lovely as it feels, I want more of him. I want to see the side of him I've witnessed before, the dominant side.

Love, In Balance

"Quin... You can do what you want with me. You take the lead. Tell me what you want and then do it" I say whilst almost moaning through the tension I feel.

"I want *you*, beneath me, on top of me and everywhere, as long as you're near me. I want to be inside of you. I want to see you. All of you" he says, almost growling.

He stops, coming to a realisation for a moment, before saying "Oh and Lista, I'm clean. I haven't been with anyone for a long time, but I got tested before and everything is clear".

"I got tested after what happened last year... I haven't been with anyone since then. I'm clear too. Thank you for caring enough to mention it Quin" I say, still so in awe of the man that is holding me right now.

"Now that's all sorted. I want you" he says, kissing my jaw and down my neck.

Our breathing gets heavier, and we rush to take each other's clothes off so our skin can meet.
He flips me over, exactly like I imagined in my fantasy, the night we kissed. He kisses and lightly bites my bare skin, tracing the line of my sternum tattoo with his tongue. It feels so good that I'm struggling to keep my moans contained. He continues kissing my skin, lowering himself further down before stopping in mid thought.

"Would you feel more comfortable taking your prosthetic off Lista?" he says, kindly but still in a sexy tone.

Why does this turn me on?
No one has ever been this considerate to think about my comfort before. Usually they're a bit creeped out by the detaching of said lower leg, but Quin just wants me to be content.

"Let's not ruin the mood. Plus my leg likes to be part of the action. I'll take her off later. Or if you feel more comfortable, I can do so now –." He puts a finger to my lips, stopping me from continuing.

"I'm happy as long as you are Lista. Let's give her some action, shall we". *Dear lord*, this is too much for my inexperienced sexual mind.
He kisses down my leg, running his hand across the pattern on my prosthesis.
"I designed it myself" I say to him.

"Prosthetic engineering is one of my favourite topics Lista. Hence why I became a biomechanical engineer. You've done an incredible job" he says, whilst kissing my leg. No one has ever done anything like this to me. It's astonishing. And the fact that he's talking to me about engineering whilst we're both here, naked. Most guys just rush straight into it. Not Quin. It's different with him.

"Now that I've given her some attention, I think *you* deserve some more, don't you think?" he says as he brings his finger up my thigh to meet my most sensitive part. I shiver and moan, arching my back as he grasps my waist with his other hand.

Love, In Balance

He circles my clit slowly, sending pleasure through my body in every direction. He replaces his finger with his tongue and continues slow circles around my bud, before running his finger down along my entrance.

I'm so wet, it's unreal. He feels it and groans.

After teasing my entrance, coating his fingers in my wetness, he pushes one finger in, and I squirm around him in pleasure.

He soon adds another finger, pumping in and out, whilst still speeding up the pace with his tongue too. It doesn't take long before I reach my limit.

I'm on the edge of my orgasm as he whispers.

"Cum for me Lista. I want to taste you on my tongue".

It's enough to push me over the edge and further, as I feel my body enter another dimension.

It's like I'm floating in a beautiful, hazed dream.

Quin removes his fingers and uses his tongue to see me through the other side of my orgasm. My body shakes and shivers through the sweet release.

He climbs up my body, so our faces meet and pecks me on the lips, smiling at my flushed skin and messy hair.

"You are the most beautiful thing I've ever seen. I've wanted to do this since New Year's Eve. I wanted to taste all of you. To make you feel incredible. I needed your body on mine" he says, moving lower and taking my breasts one by one in his mouth, sucking and licking.

I kiss his lips, deeper and wetter, before pushing him backwards onto the bed and climbing on top of him.

He gasps.

"Oh… fuck Lista" he says as I trace his ink kissed skin with my tongue, leading my way down to his erection.

I hold him in my hands and circle the swelled tip with my tongue, tasting his sweet precum, before taking him into my mouth. He groans loudly, tilting his hips and gripping the sheets as I take his full erection deep into my throat.

Once I'm used to his length and girth, I take him in faster, pursing my lips tighter to take his pleasure to the next level.

I feel his need to thrust, so I take his hand and place it at the back of my head, allowing him to find a rhythm and feel in control. It turns me on even more, knowing what he wants and when he shows me. He pumps into me at his own pace, and I can feel his erection growing.

I want him inside of me.

I make sure to merely tease, and not bring him to the edge. After I'm satisfied that he's pleased and harder than ever, I kiss up his body and meet his lips again, tasting the mixture of our arousal.

"I want you inside of me Quin" I say into his ear as I kiss his neck.

"Shall I get a condom Lista?" he asks. So considerate. What planet has he come from?

"As long as you're happy, *I* am. I'm on the pill".

"In that case" he says as he parts my legs and fills me with his erection roughly. I gasp and melt into his body as he thrusts slowly into me. I'm so desperate for more, I place both of my hands on his chest and ride him until his head falls back and he's whispering my name followed by sweet

profanities. Both of us gasping and moaning with pleasure.
He grips my ass, possessively.
It feels so good to know he wants me.

"Wow, you're so fucking tight… You feel so good". His hands loosen their grip on my ass and move up over my waist, smoothing over the skin. "You're so soft Lista, *damn*".
He flips me over so that he's above me now.
He lifts both of my legs and puts them on his shoulders, leaning towards me. He places himself at my entrance and pushes into me deeply and quick, until I'm full and moaning out loud. This position hits all the right spots and my eyes struggle to keep focus.
I whimper his name and plead for more, and he gives it to me. He fucks me hard, and I have to cover my mouth with my hand to muffle my pleasured screams.
He kisses them away when he can, but his pleasure fills him so deeply that his head lolls back often as he tries to quiet his own words.
Most people are so gentle with me, because of my leg, but Quin asks for what I want and gives it to me.
He knows I'm not delicate and he fucking treats me like a normal human being, flipping me over, lifting my legs and filling me with pleasure.
He slows the pace now, and our bodies are touching.
Chest to chest, our legs wrapped around each other's. He's holding my hands against the bed, above my head.
He's gone from fucking me, to making love to me.
We kiss deeply, passionately and it feels so intimate.
I'm taking him in deep but slow and I feel like we're the

only two people on earth. He's kissing me like he needs me to survive. I think I need him too.

Whilst still pumping into me slowly, he lifts his face, so our eyes meet, and releases my hands, bringing his to my face and hair, stroking gently.

"Lista. I'm about to say something stupid. This might be too soon, but I think I've fallen in love with you" he says, still filling me to the brim slowly with his dick.

I smile, ear to ear and kiss him, wrapping my hands around his face, stroking his jaw with my thumb. His hands are around my face too now.
He looks at me intensely, searching for my response, until his expression softens when I speak.

"Quin. I've fallen in love with you too".

We finish slowly and beautifully. Him releasing into me, filling me to the brim as I find release too.
We spend the rest of the evening cuddling, eating takeout and watching New Girl. Turns out he likes it too.
We talk about my leg, and I show him it without my prosthetic. He glides his hand across the amputation scar on my limb whilst I tell him about the history behind it. Not once did he prod, but just sat and listened. His eyes glistening.

And I know you're wondering too.
I was in a car accident with my family when I was eleven. I was the only survivor. That day I lost my mother, father and my younger brother.
My leg was crushed, but thankfully that was the only major injury I faced. My lower leg had to be removed, hence becoming an amputee.

Love, In Balance

My other broken bones could heal, and my concussion could be treated. I still suffer from balance and sensory issues due to my head injury and minor brain damage, but vestibular exercises have helped it become more manageable. My physical aids have been life savers.

The mental trauma was harder to recover from, but after therapy and living with my auntie growing up, I managed to find myself and start living, rather than just being a survivor.

My passion for engineering started when I had my first prosthetic leg. I knew I wanted to grow up learning about the work behind it so I could be the difference other amputees need in their lives.

So I set my sights on gaining knowledge and learning how to design and create different types of prosthetics.

I designed and helped create my own in recent years, and I'm so excited to continue. So… yeah. That's my story (*Basically what I told Quin*).

"You are astonishing. Just because you're *you* Lista. I can't believe I've been so lucky to have you in my life". He says.

"I'm the lucky one Quin" I say, and he shakes his head, smiling.

"We're both lucky to have found each other then. When I'm with you, balance is restored. And of all the beautiful places on this earth and beyond, there's nowhere else I'd rather be". His beautiful words provoke a thought. One I've never brought up to him. But now feels right.

"Quin. You're tattoo spoke to me the first time I saw it. What's the story behind it?" I ask, tracing it with my fingers.

He looks down at the ink on his arm and smiles.

"I've always thought it was important to find equilibrium between the heart and mind. It's difficult to find. Especially regarding the heart. I've never known or felt love, in balance. It's always been conflicting, ebbing and flowing. Until now. With you" he says. My heart speeds up at this perfect admission, because I feel exactly the same way. Finally we've both found love, in balance.

Chapter 20

One year later

Lista
Playlist: *On Melancholy Hill* - Gorillaz

Life is good. The best it's ever been to be honest.
I never thought I could find real happiness or balance in my life. But here I am.
I moved in with Quin, into his house a while ago and our kitties managed to find peace, thankfully. His house is nice and big for all the future plans we have.

Quin proposed whilst we revisited the place we met. It was absolute perfection. He did it so it was exactly a year since we'd met, and my heart is the fullest it's ever felt.
I of course said yes! We took the pubs yearly quiz. Still didn't win, but the memories made up for it.

There are so many positive things in my life right now, and incredible things to look forward to; The future of my project, having the best friends a girl could ask for, being around to see the guys and Flic live their own love stories (I can only hope Flic and Drew see sense), and of course, Oli's VIP birthday party.

The one he hasn't shut up about for the last few months. He's been so plan obsessed and has roped Five Mountains into helping, like a good friend does.

I personally can't wait to get dressed up and celebrate with incredible friends and my fiancé. Sometimes, it's the little things in life. Speaking of those incredible friends, the guys helped me file a report against Pierce, and more students came forward with similar heart-breaking stories.

He was arrested for sexual assault and harassment and has been fired from the university.

Once everything was over and he left, I started doing talks as a sexual abuse survivor and even incorporated it into my lived experience work. So many people explained how much it helped, and honestly, it feels like I'm making a difference bit by bit.

Quin and I came out about our relationship and thankfully staff and students were understanding since we met prior to becoming associated via the uni. But even if we weren't, you truly can't help who you fall in love with. And I'd have stopped at nothing to make it all ok for our us.

Some students were heartbroken to say the least, and I get some questionable looks from the ladies. I think they're jealous. Sorry, but I was here first. *Actually, not sorry.*

Quin stepped down as my advisor, but we continued a joint prosthetic engineering project off campus in our own time, which we've now turned into a little side hustle.

With both our expertise, we're now working on creating new prosthetics and bionics for young people, both with beautiful designs, and are hoping since I'm almost finished my PhD, that it can become a long-term career and business.

Love, In Balance

With Autumn surrounding us, I've been designing some spooky prosthetic looks and am also in the midst of designing and testing out prosthetic stickers, so that the young people we design for can pick and choose their own temporary seasonal designs. I might even start my own sticker company, specialising in weather resistant prosthetic friendly products.

There really is no limit to what we can do when we have passion.

I never imagined I'd be lucky enough to find myself again, and to find someone who loves me and brings such balance in love and my life. As I sit in our living room, looking to my side to see Quin cuddling kitty Edith and Edison, I realise that there truly is nowhere else I'd rather be. And everything I've ever been through has brought me to this very moment.

Quin and Lista's story may be over, but fear not, they'll be back again in the next book in the series.

Do you want to know more about the mysterious, grumpy, infuriating Si, and whether a new face tempts him to open up his buried heart? Read a sneaky preview of his story in book 2 of the Five Mountains series here!

Read ahead for a snippet of this even spicier story than book one. It's just a little chance to meet the main characters. No major spoilers! *Beta version – Final version may differ

Prologue

Si
Playlist: *Natural* – Imagine Dragons

Attending parties is not my favourite thing to do. I don't mind them, per se, but I'd rather not have the pressure of socialising on my mind. Small talk isn't exactly my forte. I enjoy getting suited and booted, and having a few drinks, but being in a room full of so many people can get a little too much.

Being around my mates is fine. I enjoy their company, catching up and just the general feeling of ease I get whilst being surrounded by them, but when you add lots of other people to the mix, I get on edge and irritated. That's why I'm

Love, In Balance

tentative about Oliver's birthday party tonight. It's not just your average gathering at a house, you see.

It's a big *'VIP themed party'*, held in a hotel hall.

A posh one too. He's not doing anything by halves, let's put it that way. I'm talking excellent quality food, fancy table décor and first drinks on the house for everybody. That's a lot of fucking drinks in my opinion.

How do I know all of this insider information? Well, it's because he got all of us from our group involved in it. He even created a special *'Five Mountains VIP Party Prep'* WhatsApp group chat and has been floating around ideas for over six months on it. From the colour scheme, to who he should invite, the cuisine that would be best to serve, and just about every fucking thing you could possibly imagine that needs to be considered for a party.

It's been... interesting to say the least. Let's also bear in mind that this isn't even a 'big' birthday in terms of his age. He's turning 33. Thirty. Three. It's just kind of a regular age. Not one that's usually up there with the sixteen, eighteen kind of celebratory ages.

I mean, when I turned 33 I just decided to have my main friends around my place for a get together. No decorations, no fancy food either. We just ordered in. No stress, no hassle. Just chill. And even that was draining. I had seven people there.

But Oliver is an eccentric guy who loves making a big deal of things. He claims that the reasons behind this extravagant, big deal is that life is hard and often pretty shitty, so he wants to make the most of the present and enjoy his birthday surrounded by his friends, acquaintances and younger members of his family. *Just to have a good drink, delicious food and help everyone forget their worries for the night.* I quote him of course, when I say that.

I can't fault the man. He's certainly not wrong with his reasoning, and I respect the sentiment behind it too. He likes to think that every birthday should be a special one. Afterall, another year of life is a big deal. We often take the years for granted I suppose and he's showing that every day, week, month and year you get to spend living deserves to be celebrated. I'm pretty sure being around him has made me softer. I definitely would not have thoughts like this without being in close proximity to him. It's just not how I work. Some call me hard; some call me grumpy. Lista just thinks I'm *'infuriating'*— to quote her. Yeah, maybe I am. It's better than wearing your heart on your sleeve though isn't it? If no one can see how I'm feeling, it's harder to break me then isn't it? I keep myself guarded for good reason and I intend to keep it that way. I'm done with disappointment and loss.

On saying all of this though, Oliver's philosophy has definitely prompted me to start thinking differently and seeing *some* things his way. Emphasis on the *some*. After everything in my life, I need to change my outlook perhaps, even if it's just short-term.

You know how much of a top guy Oliver is? *And over the top*. He's essentially planned two birthday celebrations. Well, with the extensive help of us lot. There's the VIP party for friends, acquaintances and close in age family members, and his *#birthday2.0 'VIF (Very important family) meal'* for his older family members. The man is a genius as well as being super thoughtful. His thinking was that having two shindigs would separate the wild side of his life from his family side. He definitely doesn't want his family to see his drunk friends dancing on tables I guess. Not that I will be. But I honestly cannot say who the hell he's invited. I mean, he must know a lot of people to fill an entire hotel hall. I rarely have enough friends to fill my living room.

I am secretly hoping that there will be so many people there that I can safely blend into the corner with the guys. And I can only hope no one tries to set me up.

Again.

They're super good at doing that whenever we're out and about. It's never Reed or Pippin who get targeted. To be honest, they're usually the ones on the other end of it.

Drew doesn't welcome matchmaking, so they don't even bother considering it. I'm pretty sure we all know that there's only one woman in his life who he wants, but only time will tell I suppose. So that means that Felicity is also off limits. I'm pretty sure Drew would bite our heads off if we even attempted to help Felicity find love.

Callista can't exactly get picked on, otherwise I'm pretty sure her fiancé Quin would have something to say about the matter.

Olivers love life is pretty on the down low. As eccentric as he is, he doesn't really discuss dating. He'll often make comments about someone being attractive, but in all the years I've known him, which is a fucking long time, I've never known him to bring a date around and show them off. So that leaves me. The one that everyone loves to pick on. They know I'm not interested in dating right now, but they are persistent little shits who like to meddle. They're under the impression that I need someone in my life to help me soften up a little. Or technically harden (I'm sorry. I'm not so good at jokes). I'm perfectly fine as I am though.

I work hard and *a lot*. I find getting close to people difficult and I just don't feel ready for being pushed together with someone I don't know. If it's going to happen, it'll happen naturally.

Not by being set up at random places with a stranger I have nothing in common with. I can't stand the lads, and often times Callista and Felicity pushing a woman my way whilst out and about. It's awkward and ends up with one of us making an excuse to leave the situation. I need to pop to the toilet; I may have left the hob on; Oh, sorry I have to take this call. Often times, that someone is me. So, set ups are a big no-no. Especially the ones that are hugely unplanned and done by tipsy friends.

I'll just have to trust the universe on this one; Not that I've trusted it before with how life has gone.

I think I'd rather just be alone for now. It seems like a safer bet for me. I don't expect anyone to understand, but quite frankly I don't need them to. I've always been a little misunderstood. Rightly so. My past has impacted my future self and I've been this way since my early teens.

Honestly, I think I'm hugely overthinking this party. You see what socialising in large groups does to me. It's been putting my mind into overdrive for a while now and I need to tap into my logical brain and realise how ridiculous I'm being. I'm going to be at the party, with good friends, quality food and drink, and I *will* enjoy myself. Simple. No need to worry or fret over things that are highly unlikely to happen. It's not like I'll have to stray from my comfort zone and have to play prince charming. Which I'm honestly not sure I'm physically and emotionally capable of anyway.

To be honest, after mid-afternoon today I'll be occupied by Olivers last minute party panic and then I'll be getting changed and heading to the hotel early with most of the guys for pre-drinks and a once over of the hall. I say that, but I'll mostly likely be standing there nodding and agreeing until Oliver stops obsessing and chills out.

Morning crisis averted, I head for a run along the local river to clear my head, get some fresh air and release some pent-up energy. I have to get it out some way, so exercise always helps. I grab a shower, get changed and head over to the hotel. I've been here once, when Oliver was looking around to see if it was *the one*. Turns out it was. I felt like I was picking out the perfect venue for a wedding. Certainly not for a birthday party, but here we are. And it is very nice.

For some reason, in the Autumn season it seems bigger and more lavish. It's a good job I wore my best suit. I'm not exactly one for fashion, but being Olivers friend has definitely forced me into at least being conscious of what I wear. He says I supposedly fit into the dark academia meets

Slytherin style category. I have no idea what that means, but after looking it up on Pinterest, I hate to admit that he's pretty accurate.

It's been an eventful day, and yet it's only 5pm. I've stood alongside Reed, Pippin and Drew witnessing a meltdown from Oliver which consisted of moving tables around with the staff and then realising they looked better where they were originally. None of us helped him. He needed to do this himself. If we even tried to chip in, he'd bite our heads off, so we stand to offer what some would see as moral support. In reality, we were sniggering and taking the piss out of him under our breath. All in a friendly manner of course.

Now that his crisis is averted, which takes us to two whole crises, if we include mine, which is enough for one day, we all head to Olivers room for last minute prep and a drink or two before heading down to the main hall.

"Cheers lads. Here's to celebrating another year of my life with you arseholes" Oliver says, raising his champagne glass.

We all comply and meet his glass mid-air, clinking all of our drinks together.

"Cheers" I say. I'm not a man of many words. Out loud anyway. I have enough of the fuckers in my head to write a book. On the outside I keep it to a minimum.

Drew raises his eyebrows at me for some reason, despite us toasting to Oliver.

"Cheers guys. Here's to the perfect opportunity to find Silas true love once and for all". I hate him. He's clearly initiating a set up for me to avoid him being the target, knowing that Felicity won't get here until much later in the night.

"How kind of you to bring that up" I say, offering him a swift kick to the shin. He buckles and warns me with his eyes to not do that again.

I raise my eyebrows at him, telling him without words to kindly back off. He smiles now, patting my back.

The others don't catch on though.

"Wait, Oli, didn't you say you had a few cousins coming? Maybe one of them would go nicely with Silas Slytherin over here" Reed says. Firstly, he knows I hate my full first name. Secondly, he loves to rile me up. I decide to be the mature one and not punch him in the dick.

Oliver decides against maturity though.

"Actually, Reeds right Si. There'll be some good options tonight. A few might be a bit older than you, but I'm sure they're happy to have a nice six-four toy boy" he says winking. "Or there's Magdalene, my favourite cousin. She's a bit younger but I reckon you'd get on" he says.

Before any of us could even get a word in, both Pippin and Reed ask, "Is she fit?". I hate everything about that question, so I continue to ignore them. Oliver does in fact answer though, despite it being his cousin.

"Well although beauty is in the eye of the beholder" wow, ultimate cheese "she is beautiful and yet has no idea people see her that way. I haven't seen her for a while, but she's always been one to put herself down, despite being incredible. You'll see lads. Trust me" he says, looking directly at me like he's baiting me.

We leave the room and head down to the hall just in time for everyone to start arriving in clusters.

I honestly thought I hadn't taken the bait Oliver tried to throw my way earlier, although annoyingly I'm now finding myself searching the crowd for his cousin. Fuck.

Chapter 1

Lene
Playlist: *I need something* – Newton Faulkner

I'm getting ready for my cousins birthday party, and I haven't a clue what to wear. I'm concerned that my usual attire isn't fitting enough for his rather... classy venue and more than likely classy friends. Not to say that I'm not classy, but we come from slightly different backgrounds with varying degrees of wealth. His mum/ my auntie is slightly higher up on the social ladder than my mother. They've always been a little in competition with one another. Who can have the biggest house, best job, most handsome, rich husband, nicest outfit, most successful children (*Hi. Just trying to make you proud mum. Love, Lene*). The list goes on and on. Believe me, for twenty-five years I've bared witness to it. Just sisterly competition I suppose. Although I wouldn't know, being the only child and all.

Whilst I'm lucky with my family's financial stability, I'm worried that I'll be the odd one out and just not good enough. Then again, aren't I always? *Laughs internally.*

"Adjust your camera Lene. I can't see your whole outfit!" Eli says from the screen on my phone, that's leant against my dressing table mirror. He's thankfully helping me come to my senses about what I need to wear. He is my guardian angel and to be honest, my personal stylist.

I'm extremely grateful that he's my plus one this evening, otherwise I'd be perched in a very fancy corner, sipping an overly expensive drink, looking like a lost puppy that no one wants to rescue. And let's face it, it's just not a good look.

I want to be less *'lost puppy'* and more powerful *'knows who she is'* phoenix. You know?

He looks me up and down.

"Miss Magdalene, you look divine. I could eat you up" Eli says, pretending to bite me through the camera.

"Eli let's be serious. Does it really say, 'I'm a badass, gorgeous, classy woman who totally goes to fancy parties every other weekend'?". He looks at me through the camera as if he's lost the will to live, which he does often when dealing with my antics. I do too in all honesty.

"Lene, you are the most beautiful creature I have ever met. No outfit can possibly live up to who you are as a person. But yes, it does say that, because it's on you. You look beautiful. Plus you shouldn't be trying to please everyone. Just wear what you like, what feels comfortable and what makes you feel good".

I love him. I really do. He is my rock. In another life we'd be married to one another and having beautiful babies, but I'm not so lucky. I'm not generally lucky with guys to be honest. And since I'm 25 and have never dated or been in a relationship, I don't see my luck changing anytime soon.

"Thank you Eli, but it's easy for you to say. You're a six-foot-something hunk that could be on the world's sexiest men list, so yeah" I say, with my 'told you so' face.

He laughs but he knows it's true.

He is the most confident, but least cocky person I have ever met. And he knows he's incredibly sexy. I want to be like him.

"Well, I mean, I can't deny it" he says with a wink. "Seriously though Lene, if you don't decide now, I'm coming over and dragging you out of the house, even if you're naked". He's serious. He will do that. He's done it before whilst we were in our first year of University. I've never gotten over it.

After Eli's serious threats and us both ending the video call following his much-needed advice, I finally decide on the finishing look and head out in my car to pick Eli up. I decided on a black dress that drapes over both of my shoulders, showing a little bit of cleavage and my shoulder tattoos. When I say little bit of cleavage, I mean it, since that little bit makes up most of my actual breasts.

It's a flowing sort of dress that comes to my mid-thigh. It's not very figure hugging. I like comfort you see. Plus, if there's a good buffet, I need room for my stomach to comfortably bloat. I have to look out for her you see.

She keeps me alive.

Mmm food... That's my stomach talking.

I've paired it with a long blazer that matches the length of my dress and have some classy ankle high doc martens on, because fuck fancy high heels. Am I right? I'd rather be comfortable and compromise people's opinions of my footwear, than be in pain and start eventually walking like I'm a new-born giraffe. Although they are super cute. Honestly though, what grown woman likes being referred to as cute? Because I don't.

I'm wearing my best gold jewellery, which comprises of a thick gold chain and my thick hooped earrings with a charm on each. The charms may be a little less... ordinary and classy though. My mum hates it when I wear my 'cheaper' jewellery additions. But I love them, so fuck it. I've always been different to my family. Exactly the way I like it.

Eli kisses me on the cheek as he sits in the passenger seat of my car.

"I see you've gone for the classiest of shoes" he says, raising his eyebrow.

I look at him in admiration. He is truly breathtaking in his tailored suit. He puts me to shame.

"Only the classiest my dear" I say. We both laugh. But his smile straightens when he starts to take my outfit in.

"Lene are you serious?". He is not amused.

"What have I done now your lordship? I ask, genuinely confused as to what I've done to inconvenience him.

"Why do you have your chemistry earring charms on?" he says, signalling to my earrings and shakes his head.

I'm very passionate about my style decisions. Especially when they are related to science.

"Because they're great. Why would I not!?" I say, absolutely confident in my accessories of choice. The ones my mother would despise. The dopamine and serotonin molecular structure ones. My absolute favourites.

He puts his head in his hands. I continue my inspiring rant.

"What is the point in being me if I don't express what makes me different? I'd rather someone notice me for being me, whilst I'm being true to myself" I say. Okay folks, motivation dialogue over. Cut the powerful background music.

"And this is why I love you" he says, gracing my cheek with a kiss. I drive on and put my best Autumn playlist on. It's one that Eli and I share on Spotify, so we both have equal contribution to what's on it. That way, we can both enjoy it and avoid arguing over who controls the soundtrack to whatever road trip we're on. It's an eclectic mix for sure, but it does the job. Singing along to the music definitely occupies my mind, but I'm still nervous about tonight. I can only imagine how gorgeous everyone will look, and it makes me self-conscious of my outfit choice, plus just myself in general.

Eli will fit in. He always does. Plus he'll be garnering all of the attention, so I can just sit back, and people watch until it's home time. It's what I usually do whenever I'm out anyway. I'm not the type you read about where every guy will turn their heads when I walk in. I don't think I've ever turned any heads. Ok, now I'm feeling a little out of my depth. We find a space in the hotel car park where the party is held, and I calm my nerves before Eli opens the door like the true gentleman he is, and I get out. I lock up the car, do a last-minute perfume spritz and link his arm before we walk into my cousins party. I am slightly shitting myself. Thankfully *not literally.*

Eli strides in with such confidence that it takes me back slightly. It does however help ease the growing tension in my stomach and help me feel a fake sense of confidence too. People look at us as we walk in, but I'm fully aware that they'll be gawking over the sexy giant I happen to be linking arms with. He does have that effect on people. Even teenage Eli had that exact reaction from me, and he was nowhere near as magnificent as he is now.

I take in my surroundings as best as I can whilst trying to look like I'm not trembling under the weight of peoples possible thoughts of me. The hall is unbelievably beautiful. It's definitely the perfect venue for Oliver. His mum will be proud. She's definitely beat my mother on this one. For my twenty-first birthday it was definitely not as lavish as this. Not too far off, but Oli has definitely one upped me. Not that we've ever been even close to both of our mothers antics.

I spot Oliver over the other side of the hall, talking with a group of friends. He looks insanely good. It's been a while since I last saw him, but I like to think we are still close regardless of how often we get together.

I signal to Eli to move directions, so we do.

"Oliver's over there in the far corner. Let's go and say hi" I say to him, discretely pointing to the group of men across the room. Proud to be making the first move, for once.

We start making our way over to where Oliver is standing. Nerves are building in my stomach but dissipate at the hilarity of Eli and his thought processes.

"Those guys your cousin is standing with might just be good options for you" he says with a deadly serious tone of voice but looks down at me and raises his eyebrows. I feel like an eighteenth-century daughter taking a turn around the room with her mother. The mother who is desperately trying to marry her off. It seems that Eli is more invested in pairing me up with a guy than I thought he was.

He's never pressured me, as such. But he definitely thinks I deserve love. I'm not so sure I need another man in my life, Eli takes up quite a lot of space. I'm also scared of the big elephant in the room— I've never been with anyone. No one has ever seemed interested in being with me I guess. I do a double take of all of the men standing with Oliver and shake my head.

"Are you out of your mind. None of those guys will look twice at me. Have you seen the other women here. I'll quit while I'm ahead, thanks" I say, tugging him closer and looking down at the floor, suddenly conscious of how small and insignificant I am.

Eli laughs under his breath, and I wonder why he's finding my discomfort enjoyable.

"Why are you laughing at me right now?" I say to Eli deadly serious. He continues laughing. He's starting to grate on me slightly because of how outside of the joke I feel.

"Because one of the guys who supposedly would; and I quote '*never look twice at you*' has been staring at you this whole time" he says with a smirk on his face. My eyes leave his and look to where Olivers friends are. That's when my gaze meets a certain dark pair of eyes that happen to be staring back at me.

Love, In Balance

Friend message code sheet

♥ = 1 black heart - I need help. 2 – It's urgent.

🏠 = Home symbol - I'm at home.

💖 = Sparkly heart – The date is going well.

💔 = Broken heart – The date is not going well. (You could pair this with the black heart code if needed)

🧟 = Zombie symbol - I'm hungover. (You could pair this with the black heart code if needed)

🔥 = Fire symbol – I'm pissed off and angry. Leave me alone or risk facing my wrath.

🧑‍🚒 = Fire man/ woman symbol - I'm pissed off and angry, but I want you to come help me feel better. It's safe.

⚡ = Lighting bolt - I am in danger. (You could pair this with the black heart code if needed)

📵 = Phone with a line crossing it - Don't call me. I can't speak right now.

📞 = Phone symbol - Call me as soon as possible. (You could pair this with the black heart and lightning bolt code if needed)

♡ = Blue heart – I'm ok.

Meet the author

(FYI I definitely do not look like this most of the time. Just imagine a messy bun, double chin and constant subconscious frown. That's usually me, and both sides are just as magnificent.)

Hi! I'm Louna. I'm 27 and from Birmingham, England, but in my mind, I'm in the countryside on a hill looking out at gorgeous scenery, pretending I'm in a Jane Austin Novel. I'd say on a ranch imagining I'm in an Elsie Silver book, but it's quite a distance from England (Sad face).
I'm obsessed with being cosy, wrapping up in blankets and drinking warm drinks. You'll either find me playing video

and board games or snuggled up reading a good book (or two. *Not at the same time).*

I adore writing and have written the majority of my work in coffee shops, being inspired by the people I see and the atmosphere around me.

Despite struggling with extreme anxiety, mild social phobia and being neurodiverse, I try to challenge myself and go above and beyond what my imposter syndrome makes me feel I can't do.

I'm currently a BSc (hons) Combined STEM student, hence why I love incorporating STEM careers into my novels. I believe in challenging the social norms and writing badass characters who represent real people, with real issues too.

I'm a lived experience practitioner in a university and mental health advocate, sharing my experience of having mental illness, having family with mental illness, and also of working in the social services as a kinship carer. I hope to make a difference bit by bit. I've always wanted to be a positive force in the world and drive positive change.

From a young age I used to think about stories whilst I lay in bed, to stop the spiral of anxious thoughts. I continued doing so as an adult, and then decided to put those stories in writing and create books! So here we are. You are officially reading the late-night thoughts that help me sleep. I hope my words can help you find a better headspace too and take you somewhere happy when you're struggling. That's what books are for right? Unless they're horror. But I do love a good scary story!

Anyway, I digress. I'm just a petite, nerdy book worm, writing and sharing my work with the world in hopes that someone will find them, escape from reality for a short while and most importantly, smile or cry happy tears.

Thanks for reading and being with me for this journey. I hope you're having a beautiful day, night, week, month, year. You're amazing, and I hope you know that. Stay wonderful!

Louna x

Acknowledgements

Writing and self-publishing my first book has been a mighty challenge. From writer's block and imposter syndrome, to struggling with the name of the book, it's been an up and down journey. I've laughed, been on the edge of giving up and gone on to shock myself at actually completing it. So first of all I'd like to put out into the universe that I acknowledge my own efforts.

However, all of this wouldn't have been possible without my best friend and partner too. Lewis, thank you for reading drafts, making sense of my ramblings and above all, being there for me during tough times as well as good times. You are the inspiration behind a lot of my male characters, hence why I fall in love with them all.

Thank you to my best friend and fellow book lover Avery, for being the first person to read one of my final drafts of this book. You have no idea how helpful it has been hearing how you found it. Plus having someone to talk to about it helped hugely. Thank you for always being there for me.

Thank you Mixo for designing my cover. It's more than I could hope for, honestly. You are incredibly talented and brought my vision to life. You are also a great friend, and I appreciate you so much for being in my life.

Thank you to Aaron, my talented and awesome friend and tattoo artist who kindly designed Callista's prosthetic. I love it and am very tempted to get it tattooed on myself!

Thank you to my friend group #3Canoes.

You guys inspire the group getaways I write about in books, plus have helped me with advice, potential names of the book and have just given so much support and motivation throughout.

Thank you to my friends and family who support me day to day. I don't reach out for help much, and in times of struggle, just like my main character Callista, I retreat to my little mind palace and struggle internally, but having friends around me helps me more than you'll know. The times we meet up for coffee, drinks, food, games night or adventures help me feel uplifted and keep me going.

Thank you to the coffee shops I've worked in. The staff are friendly and make delicious drinks that keep me awake and thriving. I'm forever inspired by people watching. I'm also thankful for my coffee shop friends too; In particular, the older gentleman with the brightest smile who says hi to me every time and gives me faith in humanity.

Thank you to my mum, who is my best friend and the craziest lady in my life. Despite you being mildly creeped out by sexual scenes and therefore probably can't read the book, I explained the entire story and you loved it. Your reaction made my day. You rooting for my characters and then jumping up and down when they got together really helped me feel like I'd succeeded in the happy ending I was hoping for.

Thanks also to the part of myself that, despite struggling, pushed past the intrusive, negative thoughts and said, "Fuck you, I'm going to be an incredible author!" and wrote an entire book! Drop the mic.

Love, In Balance

www.ingramcontent.com/pod-product-compliance
Ingram Content Group UK Ltd.
Pitfield, Milton Keynes, MK11 3LW, UK
UKHW021103050125
452996UK00009B/67